KILLER RIBS

Library of Congress Control Number: 2005938562

ISBN: 1-932855-37-8

Cover Photograph: Ross Durant/JupiterImages

Killer Ribs: Mouthwatering Recipes from North America's Best Rib Joints is produced by becker&mayer!, Bellevue, Washington.
www.beckermayer.com

Design: Kasey Free
Editorial: Kate Perry
Image Coordination: Nancy Davidson and Meghan Cleary
Production Coordination: Adrian Lucia
Project Management: Sheila Kamuda

10 9 8 7 6 5 4 3 2 1

Manufactured in China.

Chronicle Books LLC
85 Second Street
San Francisco, California 94105

www.chroniclebooks.com

KILLER RIBS

NANCY DAVIDSON

RIBS

Mouthwatering Recipes from North America's Best Rib Joints

CONTENTS

CANADA

NORTHEASTERN U.S.

MIDWESTERN U.S.

WESTERN U.S.

SOUTHERN U.S.

N
W E
S

06 INTRODUCTION
08 RIBS 101

NORTHEASTERN U.S.

10 Finkerman's Riverside Bar-B-Q, VT
12 Dinosaur Bar-B-Que, NY
14 Holy Smokes BBQ & Whole Hog House, MA
16 LJ's BBQ, RI
18 Uncle Willie's, CT
20 Blue Smoke, NY
22 R.U.B., NY
24 The Original Big Ed's BBQ, NJ
26 Tommy Gunn's American Barbeque, PA
28 Chubby's Barbeque, MD

MIDWESTERN U.S.

30 Roscoe's Root Beer & Ribs, MN
32 Smoky Jon's #1 BBQ, WI
34 Twin Anchors Restaurant & Tavern, IL
36 The Smoke Daddy, IL
38 Hickory Park, IA
40 Uncle Earnie's Beer, Bait, and BBQ, NE
42 Oklahoma Joe's Barbecue, KS
44 Gates Bar-B-Q, MO
46 Arthur Bryant's Barbecue, MO
48 Buffalo Bob's Smokehouse, KS

SOUTHERN U.S.

50 Dixie Bones, VA
52 Moonlite Bar-B-Q Inn, KY
54 The Original Q Shack, NC
56 Allen & Son, NC
58 The Barbecue Joint, NC
60 Cozy Corner Restaurant, TN
62 Big Bob Gibson Bar-B-Que, AL
64 The Salt Lick, TX
66 Smitty's Market, TX
68 Bubbalou's Bodacious Barbecue, FL

WESTERN U.S.

70 Jones Barbecue, WA
72 Willow Creek Café and Saloon, MT
74 Road House BBQ, ID
76 Eagle Rib Shack, ID
78 Q4U, UT
80 Memphis Minnie's, CA
82 Memphis Championship Barbecue, NV
84 Robb's Ribbs, NM
86 Joe's Real BBQ, AZ
88 Mr. K's BBQ, AZ

CANADA

90 Klondike Rib & Salmon BBQ, YT
92 Palomino Smokehouse and Social Club, AB
94 Big T's BBQ & Smokehouse, AB
96 Muddy Waters Smokehouse, MB
98 Dusty's Bar & BBQ, BC
100 Kansas City Bar.B.Q. Shack, BC
102 Memphis Blues Barbecue House, BC
104 Dix Barbecue and Brewery, BC
106 Mike Love's Barbeque & Smokehouse, ON
108 Phil's Original BBQ, ON

110 INDEX
112 RESOURCES &
     ACKNOWLEDGEMENTS

INTRODUCTION

It's often said that your favorite barbecue is the one you grew up with, and that you spend your life comparing all other barbecue to the ideal smoked meat of your childhood. When I was growing up in the suburbs of New York City, my dream barbecue was Chinese spareribs with a thin layer of sweet, tangy sauce and chicken slathered with bottled sauce, charred on the backyard grill. I had my first taste of Southern-style barbecue when I went to college in Philadelphia. My boyfriend at the time loved to go for ribs with me because he always got to eat my order as well as his—I just didn't get it.

The barbecue bug bit me at the Big Apple Barbecue Block Party in New York City. It was there that I first began to learn about authentic barbecue. The meat was cooked low and slow over indirect heat and wood smoke. After that, I was itching to understand the regional differences—Texans prefer beef; North Carolina is famous for a vinegar-based sauce; South Carolinians add mustard to their sauce; Kansas City has a reputation for pork ribs with a sweet-and-sticky sauce; and Memphis is known for their paprika-based dry rub.

That block party opened my eyes and my taste buds. Now that I've tasted barbecue from all over the barbecue belt, I can tell you that every region has something unique and tasty to offer. It would be a shame to let regional pride cause you to miss out on any of them.

And in fact, when it comes to ribs the borders are not so clearly delineated. In tracing the growing interest in barbecue around North America, I found that the sauce at the most famous Kansas City joints is not so

sweet and not so sticky, and that some North Carolina joints serve Texas-style pork ribs.

As barbecue spots pop up from the far reaches of the Yukon Territory to the urban jungle of Manhattan, regional differences take on new meaning. Some newcomers pay homage to all the regions, providing neophytes with a spectrum of barbecue flavors. One town in Idaho—not a state known for its barbecue—plays host to two 'cue joints where transplants from two very different barbecue backgrounds now make their homes. I found that Memphis-style, dry-rubbed ribs have caught the fancy of some very serious pit masters in San Francisco and Vancouver. I found a "dive" in Florida that makes great pork ribs and also serves up alligator ribs for a special treat, as well as a place in Kentucky that specializes in mutton ribs, maintaining

a centuries-old tradition at their forty-plus-year-old restaurant. I also found championship pit masters who frequently engage in rib cook-off competitions, and other champions who focus only on their customers.

Many of the pit masters from outside the traditional barbecue belt first experienced "real" barbecue when they traveled throughout the southern United States on business. They were so intrigued by what they tasted that they eventually changed careers. In other cases, classically trained restaurateurs studied generations-tested barbecue techniques before experimenting with their own. Other pit masters have a genetic connection to barbecue, tracing their barbecue roots to Georgia and Oklahoma, Missouri and Arkansas. But however they came to it, these pit masters all have one primary thing in common: They make killer ribs!

RIBS 101

Prepping the Ribs

Demembraning

Almost as controversial as what region produces the best ribs is whether to remove the membrane on the back of ribs. Many say that demembraning your ribs will allow the smoke and flavor to penetrate the meat, but others contest that the membrane will keep the meat on the bones and that it's not worth the trouble to remove it. If you choose to remove it, you can ask your butcher to do it for you or you can cut and peel the membrane off by hand. These handy instructions are courtesy of Chris Lilly of Big Bob Gibson in Decatur, Alabama:

★ Place the slab of ribs bone side down on the table. Slide your knife under the membrane and against the end bone to separate the two. With a dry paper towel or rag, grasp the edge of the thin membrane and pull. The entire membrane should separate from the rib.

You can also boil the ribs for one to two hours until the membrane starts to peel away and the meat becomes tender.

Boiling

Some home cooks (and the occasional professional) will boil ribs prior to smoking, grilling, or baking. This can be a quick five-to-ten-minute parboil, just to loosen the membrane and make it easy to remove; or it can mean covering a pan full of a rack of ribs with liquid and baking it for two hours in the oven until the meat is tender. For those who choose to boil, it's only a first step—the ribs should still be finished with spices and sauce, on the grill or in the smoker. However, most long-time pit masters warn against boiling the ribs, as much of the fat—and hence the flavor—boils away. And while some prefer meat that's falling off the bone, a majority of the pit masters we spoke with argue that

ribs should have a pleasant tug and a slightly firm texture, and that it should require some effort to pull the meat from the bone.

Flavors

Regional differences often come down to distinctive spices and sauces. The recipes in *Killer Ribs* include dry rubs, marinades, mops, and barbecue sauces.

Dry rubs

A dry rub is a mixture of dry ingredients—usually salt, sugar, and other dry spices, and occasionally dry herbs—that are rubbed directly on the meat before cooking. A dry rub is also referred to as a dry marinade. Some pit masters recommend rubbing the rub into the meat so it deeply penetrates the flesh, while others recommend sprinkling it on lightly so the pores don't get clogged. In Texas-style barbecue, they tend to use just salt, black pepper, and red pepper or paprika, while some barbecue competitors might use twenty-nine different spices to flavor their rub. Some aficionados recommend letting the spices sit on the meat overnight or for 24 hours, while others call for putting the meat on the heat as soon as you finish applying the rub.

Marinades

A marinade is usually a combination of wet ingredients and spices. It can be similar to a barbecue sauce with ingredients such as tomato and vinegar, or it may actually be a thinner version of sauce. The ribs are usually covered with a marinade and left to sit for anywhere from one to 24 hours, depending on whose recipe it is. The marinade can also be used to keep the meat moist during cooking, although typically a mop is used in barbecue for this purpose.

Mops

A mop is used throughout the cooking process to keep the meat moist. It's called a mop because professional pit masters often use a mop-like implement to spread the liquid over the meat, but you can also use a spray bottle. The mop can be a combination of apple cider, water, and vinegar, or other liquid ingredients, with or without spices, or a sauce with water added.

Barbecue Sauces

Whether tomato-based or vinegar-based, used as a marinade before grilling, slathered on while smoking, added just at the end and caramelized on the grill, served on the side, or eschewed all together, it's often the sauce that makes the biggest difference when barbecuing ribs. When a recipe in *Killer Ribs* calls for barbecue sauce and there's no recipe for it, you may be able to find the sauce for sale on the restaurant's web site, but you can also use your favorite recipe from elsewhere in the book or substitute a high-quality bottled sauce from your favorite barbecue joint. You can add your favorite alcohol (Jack Daniel's works well), spices, seasonings, or citrus juice—feel free to experiment!—to a bottled sauce for extra-intense flavors.

Cooking Methods

Yet another debate is which cooking method to use. Today, a majority of restaurants use a gas-started smoker (like those produced by Southern Pride or Ole Hickory) that cooks the meat with low-temperature, indirect heat generated by wood smoke. (Direct heat is when you cook the meat at high temperatures directly over the fire, as on a backyard grill.) But some purists argue that authentic barbecue requires a pit that burns only wood. And some restaurants, like the extremely popular Twin Anchors in Chicago, don't use any wood at all.

Lucky for those of us without a real smoker, there are several ways to replicate the low-heat, slow-smoked method at home, both indoors and out:

Indoor smoking, using your stovetop and oven

This convenient method is courtesy of Dusty's in Whistler, British Columbia:

★ Create your own smoker by using a disposable aluminum pan. Fill the pan with wood chips and water, soaking the chips until they're damp. Cover the pan with foil, and put it on your stove burner on medium heat until the chips are smoldering. Then, put the meat on the upper rack of your oven and place the pan full of the smoldering chips in the bottom of your oven. Poke a hole in the foil covering the pan so smoke can escape and infuse your ribs with smoky flavor.

Outdoor grilling, using a gas grill

This useful method is courtesy of Memphis Blues in Vancouver, British Columbia:

★ Purchase one package of wood chips—Memphis Blues prefers hickory—and a smoker box at your local hardware store. Soak the wood chips in water for twenty minutes. Drain the water and place the wet chips in the smoker box. Place the smoker box on one side of your grill; turn the burners on medium-high heat—300 to 325 degrees—only on the side of the grill where the smoker box is placed. Then place the meat on the opposite, unheated side of the grill so you're cooking the meat with indirect heat.

Types of Wood

Tastes vary regarding the type of wood used as well. Most pit masters choose a wood that is indigenous and plentiful in their area—apple wood in Calgary and Illinois, oak in California, hickory in Iowa, mesquite in Texas, a blend of hickory and oak in Kansas City, and a mixture of oak, hickory, pecan, and apple in New Mexico. Whichever wood you prefer, your ribs will be infused with a delicious, mouthwatering flavor.

NORTHEASTERN U.S.
★ KILLER RIBS ★

FINKERMAN'S RIVERSIDE BAR-B-Q

MONTPELIER, VERMONT

When you think of Vermont, you're more likely to conjure up images of maple syrup and holistic vegetarian delights than racks of baby back ribs. But husband and wife team Richard Fink and Lee Duberman (Finkerman's is an amalgam of their two names) didn't see any reason that residents of the Green Mountain State should be deprived of smoked meat. Duberman, a graduate of the Culinary Institute of America, moved to Vermont to teach at the New England Culinary Institute and met Fink, also a transplant. Duberman is the chef in the family, Fink is the resident wine maven, while Duberman's sister,

Laura Fontaine, handles the day-to-day operations at Finkerman's. They also offer up live music in the best barbecue tradition on Wednesday nights.

Located in a refurbished warehouse off a bumpy road, the enclosed eating porch overlooks an overgrown river. The pork ribs showcase Duberman and Fink's research, traveling and eating barbecue in the South. The side dishes reflect Duberman's culinary training through a Southern filter: delectable Vermont cheddar macaroni and cheese, piquant jalapeno cheese grits, vegetarian black beans, fried-to-goodness hush puppies, and mouthwatering, slightly sweet cornbread.

Finkerman's Bar-B-Q Sauce

Lee Duberman isn't shy about letting you know how delicious her sauce is. Though the sauce really is something special, she isn't coy about sharing the recipe, either.

3 cups ketchup

1 cup cider vinegar

2 tablespoons soy sauce or tamari

1 tablespoon powdered mustard

$^1\!/_2$ tablespoon black pepper

$^1\!/_2$ tablespoon ancho chile powder

$^1\!/_2$ tablespoon granulated garlic

$^1\!/_2$ tablespoon granulated onion

$^1\!/_3$ cup brown sugar

$^1\!/_3$ cup molasses

$^1\!/_2$ tablespoon chipotle chile powder

1 cup water

$^1\!/_2$ tablespoon salt

Combine all ingredients in a stainless steel pot. For a spicier sauce, add an additional $^1\!/_2$ teaspoon ancho chile powder, $^1\!/_2$ teaspoon chipotle chili powder, $^1\!/_2$ teaspoon cayenne pepper, and $^1\!/_2$ teaspoon brown sugar.

Cook over a low flame for about an hour. The sauce should barely simmer, and will thicken slightly. Cool and pour into jars to store in your refrigerator for up to one week. Sauce covers 3 racks of ribs.

GENERAL COOKIN' TIPS

★ Smoke spareribs for five hours, and baby backs for three, at approximately 200 to 225 degrees, depending on size. Duberman likes to smoke over a combination of apple and cherry woods.

★ For a nice glaze, lightly coat the ribs with barbecue sauce after smoking, and finish on a direct flame on the grill for a few minutes.

DINOSAUR BAR-B-QUE

SYRACUSE, NEW YORK

In 1983, John Stage and two friends, bikers following their urge to travel, wanted to pay their way though motorcycle shows and festivals by feeding other bikers, and so they started a mobile 'cue concession stand. By the time Stage decided to settle down in Syracuse with a take-out joint in 1988, he had survived and conquered a crash course in barbecue. At the time, "barbecue in the East meant something else," says Stage. "It was what you put on the backyard grill." Though it was slow going at first, it wasn't long before the locals caught on and Stage needed more space. In 1990, with new partners Nancy and Larry Luckwaldt, Stage turned Dinosaur into a full-service restaurant with a bar and live blues music almost every night of the week. The bar has an awesome selection of beers, including a smoked porter, as well as a fitting selection of bourbons.

The connection between barbecue and bikers is clear in Syracuse, where the original Dinosaur joint is located under a local motorcycle shop, and there's never a shortage of hogs parked outside. The ribs at Dinosaur Bar-B-Que are "our reason for being," Stage says, and he points out that there are really just three ingredients: wood fire, spice, and meat.

Mutha Sauce

1 cup minced onion

$^1/_2$ cup minced green pepper

1 jalapeno pepper, finely chopped

$^1/_4$ cup vegetable oil

Pinch kosher salt

Pinch black pepper

2 tablespoons minced garlic

1 28-ounce can tomato sauce

2 cups Heinz ketchup

1 cup water

$^3/_4$ cup Worcestershire sauce

$^1/_2$ cup cider vinegar

$^1/_4$ cup lemon juice

$^1/_4$ cup molasses

$^1/_4$ cup hot sauce

$^1/_4$ cup spicy brown mustard

$^3/_4$ cup packed dark brown sugar

1 tablespoon chili powder

2 teaspoons coarsely ground black pepper

$^1/_2$ teaspoon ground allspice

Sauté the onion, green pepper, and jalapeno in vegetable oil over medium-high heat in a large saucepan until the onions are golden and soft, about 5 to 7 minutes. Season with salt and pepper. Add garlic and cook for 1 minute. Add the remaining ingredients, bring to a boil, then lower heat and simmer for 10 minutes. Store the sauce in your refrigerator until you're ready to use it (it will keep for one week), then slather it on the ribs once you're ready to serve them. Sauce flavors 4 racks of ribs.

GENERAL COOKIN' TIP

★ Get to know your butcher: Ask for meaty ribs without "shiners," bones where the meat was scraped off.

HOLY SMOKES BBQ & WHOLE HOG HOUSE

— WEST HATFIELD, MASSACHUSETTS —

Aptly named, Holy Smokes is housed in a deconsecrated Lutheran church, which owners Leslie and Lou Ekus (a.k.a. PapaLu) took over in 2004. They kept the original pews for seating and rechristened the pulpit a wait station. Leslie's son, Seth Crawford, a graduate of the Culinary Institute of America, is the executive chef and partner in the business.

Pit master PapaLu's first barbecue revelation took place at a professional food conference when a whole barbecued hog was carted in on a wooden trough, and the crowd was invited to start picking pork from the carcass. As if a divine intervention, Ekus heard a very tall women next to him say, "This is very delicious." When he turned toward her, he realized he was standing next to Julia Child. That surreal experience—and the sublime hog—opened Ekus's eyes to what barbecue could be.

For barbecue purists, they'll serve the ribs naked, but who wants to miss out on made-from-scratch sauces? There's an original sauce, a thick, sweet and tangy sauce with lots of vinegar and pure cane syrup; chipotle sauce with peppers added; sweet maple-bourbon sauce; and Batch 666, a super spicy sauce for people who want to "hurt real bad," made with cinnamon, cocoa, and habaneros for a rich, deep flavor.

Beef Short Ribs

½ cup salt

1 tablespoon black pepper

1½ tablespoons garlic powder (Holy Smokes prefers granulated garlic powder
   for "less sneezin' when you season.")

1 rack beef short ribs

Holy Smokes's recipe for ribs is quite simple, as they use the same seasoning for all the meats. Instead of using a rub, they combine salt, pepper, and garlic powder together and sprinkle it lightly over the meat before it goes in the smoker. PapaLu just wants the seasoning to bring out the natural flavor and sweetness of the meat; he avoids paprika because he thinks it "completely obliterates the flavor of the meat."

GENERAL COOKIN' TIPS

★ Smoke beef ribs in three separate pieces, still connected, for 8 to 10 hours at 200 to 210 degrees. The meat will tighten up after just a short period of time in the smoker and start to feel hard. It will stay that way for 6 to 7 hours; then, the meat gets very soft, all at once. You know they're done if you poke the ribs with your finger and find no resistance. Remember, not all ribs smoke at the same rate, so you need to test every piece and only take them out when they are done.

★ At Holy Smokes, they smoke their ribs over red oak and apple wood. The apple helps the smoke penetrate the meat better. Ekus isn't a fan of either hickory or mesquite, because he thinks the flavor is too strong. "Good barbecue is about wood flavor enhancing the flavor of the meat. You want to taste the wood in the meat, not the smoke."

★ Ekus finishes his ribs in a 900-degree wood-burning oven. After he pulls a rack of ribs out of the smoker, he glazes the meat with sauce, and caramelizes the sauce in the wood-burning oven.

NORTHEASTERN U.S. ★ KILLER RIBS ★

LJ'S BBQ

PAWTUCKET, RHODE ISLAND

There are two LJs who lent their names to this New England barbecue joint. One is Miss Leola Jean, co-owner Bernie Watson's late grandmother, who hailed from North Little Rock, Arkansas. She was a grand cook whose traditional Southern cooking inspired much of the grub here. The other LJ is Linda Jane Watson, LJ's other co-owner and Bernie's wife, who manages the front of the house while Bernie minds the pit, and also makes the tasty cornbread, succulent pies, and pickles. The restaurant looks as close to a Southern roadside joint as they could make it, except, as Linda points out, you "can't do a dirt floor" in Rhode Island. You order up at the counter and then sit at long, linked tables where 'cue lovers from

diverse backgrounds—"lawyers to Latin kings"—can't help but start up conversations, exchanging stories and phone numbers.

Linda and Bernie make just one kind of sauce: mild and tomato-based, from a family recipe that Bernie developed with his uncle, which they bottle and sell in-house. Bernie also learned his celebrated barbecuing technique from his uncle on visits back to Arkansas. When Linda first visited with him, she had her first taste of real barbecue; like other New Englanders, she confused barbecue with grilling. Now Linda and her husband are on a mission to teach their neighbors that "barbecue is a technique, not a sauce," and that it's the "only true American cuisine."

LJ's Pork Rib Rub

4 tablespoons packed light brown sugar

3 tablespoons onion powder

3 tablespoons garlic powder

2 tablespoons dry mustard

3 tablespoons paprika

1 tablespoon Bell's Seasoning

2 tablespoons dried thyme

2 tablespoons chili powder

1 tablespoon black pepper

1 tablespoon salt

Mix all the ingredients and store in a resealable plastic bag. When you're ready to use, sprinkle 2 tablespoons of the mixture on one slab of pork ribs and massage into the meat. Wrap the ribs in plastic wrap and place in the refrigerator for 24 hours, to allow the rub to tenderize the meat.

GENERAL COOKIN' TIPS

★ At LJ's, they smoke St. Louis baby backs and beef short ribs over a combination of apple and hickory wood for anywhere from 2 to 16 hours. They use their basic rub and sauce on everything, but change the cooking time depending on the meat.

★ Watson finds that there's no need for a wet mop, as there's enough moisture in the smoker to keep the ribs moist and tender.

★ The ribs are cooked completely in the smoker, but Bernie finishes them off on the grill to caramelize the rub, and then tops them with sauce.

UNCLE WILLIE'S

WATERBURY, CONNECTICUT

"Connecticut is not exactly a major barbecue state; in fact, the entire Northeast is barbecue deprived," note Jane and Michael Stern, road food warriors and frequent contributors to *Gourmet* magazine, in a roundup of the ten best barbecue restaurants in the country. But they contend that Uncle Willie's—a relative old-timer by East Coast standards—stands out as a tasty exception.

Owner Bill Lombardi (Uncle Willie himself) was bitten by the barbecue bug while traveling down South for business over the course of three or four years. He was frustrated that he couldn't find anything like it on the East Coast—with the notable exception of the now-defunct Pearson's in New York. Lombardi and his wife, Diane, became regulars at Pearson's, visited 'cue joints from Georgia to Kansas City, and started to dream about how they would do things at their own place. For two years, they developed recipes and in late 1994, they converted a deli into a Southern-style rib joint, with a counter and indoor picnic tables.

Uncle Willie's has several smokers going all the time, smoking shoulders and brisket at night and ribs in the morning. He dry rubs the ribs with a Memphis-style seasoning and doesn't add any sauce while they're smoking. The most popular sauce—served on the side—is the Memphis Classic, closely followed by the Wichita Falls Hot, but you can also choose Carolina Mustard or Lexington Vinegar.

Uncle Willie's Dry Rub

Uncle Willie's dry rub will add spice and zest to any slab of ribs!

3 tablespoons paprika

3 tablespoons dry mustard

1 tablespoon black pepper

1 tablespoon kosher salt

1 tablespoon cayenne pepper

1 teaspoon ground nutmeg

Combine all ingredients in a small bowl. Gently rub the mixture into 2 racks of ribs, on both sides, at least 3 to 5 hours in advance, and place in the refrigerator.

GENERAL COOKIN' TIPS

★ Select the best pork or beef available, and use real wood to smoke your meat. Cook indirectly at a low temperature (200 to 225 degrees) for 3 to 5 hours, depending on size of the ribs, to let the heat and smoke, not the flame, cook the meat.

★ Lombardi puts a lot of work into his meaty St. Louis–cut ribs and flavorful Texas beef ribs, smoking them over hickory and oak for hours until the meat falls off the bone. You'll notice the distinctive deep red-rose layer around the meat—the smoke ring that's the sign of real pit barbecue.

★ Have patience! Real barbecue takes time, and has to be tended. And, remember this advice from Lombardi, "To cook real pit barbecue, you must use all your senses."

NORTHEASTERN U.S. ★ KILLER RIBS ★

BLUE SMOKE

NEW YORK, NEW YORK

Although New York City has had a few barbecue restaurants—most notably Virgil's and Pearson's—it wasn't until red-hot restaurateur Danny Meyer and his Union Square Hospitality Group opened Blue Smoke that Manhattanites really started paying attention to regional barbecue. Meyer also launched the annual Big Apple Barbecue Block Party, inviting barbecue champions from the South and Midwest to strut their stuff, and served up mouthwatering dishes to the smoked meat-deprived masses that gathered in Madison Square Park.

Blue Smoke's urban take on a rib joint offers comfort and amenities, including real plates and cutlery, as well as a well-stocked bar that includes wine, champagne, tequila, and of course barbecue staples such as beer and bourbon. Before they opened Blue Smoke, Danny Meyer, chef Kenny Callaghan, and other members of their team visited the country's finest pit masters, tasting and learning everything they could about barbecue. They also consulted with Memphis in May three-time champion Mike Mills. The result is a menu that includes ribs from all over the map: lean baby back ribs served up Memphis style, saucy Kansas City ribs, and Texas-style beef ribs. On the road, Meyer says, he learned that time is an essential ingredient in making good barbecue; not just in terms of how long you smoke the meat, but in the years of experience you have making it. So while Blue Smoke is justly proud of their ribs, Meyer and Callaghan know they'll only get better over time.

Blue Smoke Black Pepper Beef Ribs

The beef ribs at Blue Smoke are big, meaty, and generous, and strictly Texas style. That means they're rubbed only with butcher-ground black pepper (coarsely ground in uniform chunks that won't melt into the food), salt, brown sugar, and paprika, and served with no sauce.

Rub
>   **2 tablespoons butcher-ground black pepper**
>   **1 tablespoon kosher salt**
>   **1 tablespoon packed dark brown sugar**
>   **1 teaspoon Spanish paprika**

2 racks beef ribs

Combine all ingredients in a bowl, mixing well to break up the brown sugar. Remove the skin from the back of the ribs with a knife (or ask your butcher to do it for you), and coat both sides of the beef ribs evenly with the rub.

Place the ribs in your oven or smoker and cook at 200 degrees for 5 $\frac{1}{2}$ to 6 hours, or until tender. Serve them immediately or wrap individually in plastic wrap and refrigerate. Refrigerated beef ribs will last up to 2 days in the refrigerator; then, to serve, simply reheat in the oven or on the grill.

GENERAL COOKIN' TIP

★ For those who want to try pork ribs, pit master Callaghan is partial to baby backs, and he recommends that you look for a leaner rib. "You don't need extra fat," he says, but because they're lean, they're also the toughest to cook. You have to wait a long time for the connective tissue to reach 180 degrees, and for the fibers to break down and start to get tender. Once that happens, you have to stop the cooking process immediately.

NORTHEASTERN U.S. · KILLER RIBS

R.U.B.

NEW YORK, NEW YORK

F or years, barbecue champion Paul Kirk traveled around the world, winning 425 cooking awards and teaching his craft to professional chefs and avid amateurs. But Andrew Fischel—one of his passionate devotees—decided he wanted to open a barbecue restaurant in Manhattan. After a few years trailing Kirk on the barbecue circuit, Fischel convinced Kirk to join him as his partner in opening R.U.B. (Righteous Urban Barbecue).

The menu at R.U.B. represents the best of Kirk's experience and twenty-five years of competitions. "We serve old-time championship-style barbecue, pulled straight out of the pit," says Fischel. Even though Kirk has been dubbed the "Kansas City Baron of Barbecue," he doesn't use the sticky, sweet sauce associated with

Kansas City at R.U.B. He and Fischel prefer to serve the meat dry, but provide sauce on request. "If they want to ruin good barbecue with a good barbecue sauce, we let 'em," says Kirk.

In fact, Kirk and Fischel don't use regional labels to describe their barbecue. The region they're most concerned about is the one on the pig. The menu distinguishes between spareribs from the tender short end (the last seven ribs off the slab), the meatier long end (the first six ribs), the rib tip (meaty upper part), and the baby back (the loin ribs). The quirky specialty of the house, dreamed up by the duo in the middle of the night during a competition-induced delirium, are deep-fried ribs, hickory smoked for five hours, covered with their secret blend of spices, dry battered, and then fried.

Paul Kirk's Dry Rub

Kirk grew up with pork spareribs and recommends them because they are more forgiving, meatier, and more flavorful than loin or baby backs. The best thing about this recipe is that you can adapt it to your taste by substituting your favorite spices for the last four ingredients.

1 cup white sugar

$1/3$ cup garlic salt

$1/3$ cup seasoned salt

$1/4$ cup onion salt

3 tablespoons celery salt

$1/2$ cup sweet Hungarian paprika

3 tablespoons chili powder

2 tablespoons finely ground black pepper

1 tablespoon lemon pepper

2 teaspoons dry mustard

1 teaspoon ground ginger

1 teaspoon ground allspice

1 teaspoon chipotle powder

Combine all of the ingredients and blend well. Store in an airtight container in a cool, dry place. This rub will season 12 racks of ribs.

GENERAL COOKIN' TIPS

★ Trim the ribs: Remove the membrane and excess fat from the back of the ribs (or ask your butcher to do it for you) to allow more seasoning and smoke to penetrate the meat.

★ At R.U.B., they slather the rack in mustard and pickle juice, then sprinkle the dry rub all over ribs just before cooking. "Vigorous rubbing clogs the pores," says Fischel. "You want the meat to cook out and the fat to render and combine with the spice and cook into the meat." You can also spray the meat with apple juice to keep it moist once it's been on the heat for a while.

THE ORIGINAL BIG ED'S BBQ

OLD BRIDGE, NEW JERSEY

When customers first meet Big Ed Stoppiello, they're usually surprised that he isn't larger. But while he may not have the girth you'd expect from someone with that name, the portion sizes he dishes out certainly are big. For starters, every day at Big Ed's BBQ is an all-you-can-eat day, featuring all the baby back ribs you can possibly fit in your stomach—which translates to 210,000 pounds of baby backs each year.

From the time he was two years old watching his father working hard, whether catering or in the family submarine sandwich shop, Stoppiello knew his future was in the food industry. It was barbecue, however, that truly captured his imagination, and his first experience was on road trips with his family as a young boy. En route to Florida from up north, they would stop in the Carolinas or Georgia for some authentic, backcountry 'cue.

Even when Big Ed's first opened, there weren't too many restaurants for first-rate barbecued ribs in the Northeast, but now you know you're in the right place the minute you drive into this spot's parking lot. The stand-alone building looks more like a roadhouse than an eatery you'd find in New Jersey, and the big tractor, Western wagons, and wheelbarrows parked outside, plus the wood-paneled interior of the joint, all add to the flavor. But you've truly arrived once you bite into those tasty baby back ribs, hot off the grill and inspired by good ole Southern cookin'.

Big Ed's Marinade

This marinade is delicious on any kind of pork, including spareribs and baby back ribs.

4 tablespoons soy sauce
4 tablespoons hoisin sauce
3 tablespoons dry sherry
2 tablespoons vegetable oil
4 teaspoons honey
2 cloves garlic, minced

Mix all the ingredients in a bowl. Allow 1 slab of ribs to marinate in the concoction for 3 hours before baking, grilling, or broiling.

GENERAL COOKIN' TIPS

★ Cook slow and low, as excess heat will dry out your ribs. Marinating will also help keep the ribs moist and juicy. In addition, at Big Ed's, they apply their sauce frequently while cooking so that it penetrates the meat and adds a distinctive flavor.

★ If you can't cook with wood, liquid smoke will give you a nice, smoldering flavor. Add it to your rib marinade and favorite barbecue sauce before and during grilling.

TOMMY GUNN'S AMERICAN BARBEQUE

PHILADELPHIA, PENNSYLVANIA

If you're looking for Tommy Gunn, you won't find him in the kitchen. The name is a tribute to an old navy chef who had a reputation for first-rate barbecue. Business partners Michael Usowski and Tommy Miller, together with executive chef Eddie Vann, transformed an "old, left for dead" gas station on the edge of Fairmont Park into an authentic barbecue joint. Vann traces his BBQ roots to Georgia and grandfather Junius "Big Tump" Doughtry. Legend has it that Big Tump used to gather with like-minded pit masters in Memphis in the 1970s to compete for best-barbecue bragging rights years before it became the site of the official Memphis in May World Championship Barbecue Cooking Contest. Big Tump also taught his daughter, Julie, how to barbecue, and she passed what she learned down to her son Eddie, who turned a family tradition into a vocation.

Tommy Gunn's meats—Philly-style spareribs, Kansas City-style baby back ribs, Carolina-style pulled pork, and Texas beef brisket—are slow-smoked daily in hickory pits and served with original, handmade barbecue sauces and an assortment of fresh homemade sides including spicy collard greens, Texas baked beans, and Chef Eddie's deep-fried macaroni. What makes their ribs Philly style? In the spirit of backyard Philadelphia cookouts, the smoked ribs are finished on the grill and slathered with Tommy Gunn's famous sauce.

Cherry Coke BBQ Sauce

Executive chef Eddie Vann is pleased to share a recipe for sauce you can make at home and slather on just about anything!

2 cups ketchup

$\frac{1}{4}$ cup cider vinegar

$\frac{1}{4}$ cup liquid smoke

2 teaspoons coarsely ground black pepper

2 teaspoons onion powder

1 teaspoon garlic powder

1 teaspoon kosher salt

2 teaspoons packed brown sugar

1 cup Cherry Coke

1 tablespoon corn syrup

Combine all ingredients in a saucepan, and place over high heat. Bring to a boil, stirring constantly with a wooden spoon. Once boiling, reduce the temperature and simmer for several minutes until sauce has thickened. Flavors 2 racks of ribs.

GENERAL COOKIN' TIPS

★ St. Louis–style ribs are trimmed so that all the ribs are exactly the same size for even cooking; when cut, they should resemble a neatly drawn rectangle. The ribs are uniform in size, but there's a lot of waste in this process because so much has to be cut away. At Tommy Gunn's, they only remove a small part of the breastbone, so the ribs vary in size. It's more of a challenge to cook them this way: "This is the real art of barbecue," says Vann—you end up with short end ribs and long end ribs, larger ribs and smaller ribs, but ultimately, much more meat on the bone.

★ Rub the meat down at least 12 hours before smoking. Smoke for 3 to 4 hours over hickory wood, or a mixture of apple, cherry, and pecan woods for a really nice flavor.

CHUBBY'S BARBEQUE

EMMITSBURG, MARYLAND

Not far from Gettysburg, Pennsylvania, there's an old-fashioned rib joint that Washingtonians find worthy of a road trip. Though the old cinder block building has been there since the late 1950s, first as a burger joint, then a roadhouse, it's only been Chubby's since 2002. Owner Tom Caulfield, who hails from Chevy Chase, Maryland, completely renovated the interior of the building, but purposely left it funky. "You don't want to go into a barbecue joint and sit in a leather banquette," he says.

Caulfield decided to make 'cue, the "most American food of all," because it's fun to fix, and more like a social event than work—plus there was no barbecue joint in the area. He started reading about it and practicing, and realized that the key to good 'cue is consistency. He serves up his dish on paper plates in gigantic portions. His food is intentionally "ridiculously fattening, which translates into ridiculously delicious." He cooks his ribs once a day and tries to make enough so that he doesn't run out. He loves ribs because they taste great and make a perfect complement to beer. But above all, Caulfield loves the kudos. "You don't have to be Bobby Flay to make good barbecue," he says, "but you have to have the passion and ego for it." He keeps a book that people sign on the way out, encouraging comments. "If I was doing this for money, I'd probably be about half as good as I am," he says. "I do it for people saying 'These are the best ribs I've ever had.' "

Hawaiian Ribs

This delicious recipe—one of Caulfield's favorites—is perfect for baking in your oven.

3 pounds pork ribs

Salt and pepper

1 cup chopped onions

2 cups green peppers, finely chopped

1 to 1½ cups tomato sauce

2 tablespoons Worcestershire sauce

⅓ to ½ cup red wine vinegar

½ cup packed brown sugar

2 tablespoons original Grey Poupon mustard

2 cans pineapple chunks, including juice

Bake the ribs in the oven at 450 degrees for 30 minutes. Remove the ribs from the oven and pour off accumulated fat. Season with salt and pepper; mix the remaining ingredients together, and spread on top of meat. Cook at 350 degrees, while checking on them and moving them around, until they are fork-tender. The longer you cook the ribs, the better, but cook for at least 3 to 4 hours. If time allows, turn the temperature down to 250 degrees and cook longer. Total cooking time will depend on how big and thick the ribs are.

GENERAL COOKIN' TIPS

★ Don't mask the flavor of meat with sauce. "I want people to taste the ribs and then decide what kind of sauce," says Caulfield. (Lots of customers even eat them dry.) Chubby's starts their classic sauce with ketchup, sugar, and salt, and then adds brown sugar, cumin, chili, garlic, salt, white and black pepper, Spanish paprika, dry mustard, and Worcestershire sauce.

★ "Smoke is a condiment," says Caulfield, "You want to feature the pork, not suck on a burnt log. It's insane to smoke for eight hours—after a couple of hours in the smoke, you are maxed out. If it ain't smoked within three and a half hours, it ain't goin' to be smoked."

ROSCOE'S ROOT BEER & RIBS

ROCHESTER, MINNESOTA

When Steve "Roscoe" Ross and his wife, Barbara, took over an A&W Root Beer drive-through restaurant to house their blazin' barbecue they painted it bright orange, but they kept the A&W menu. Without those corn dogs, onion rings, and homemade root beer during the early years, Ross doubts that he'd still be in business. He's the first to admit that his first attempts at barbecuing ribs were not stellar. "I doubt I had any repeat customers from that time. It took me a long time to learn," he says. "Those first years were scary."

But that work has paid off. Beginning in 1993, Roscoe's BBQ Rib Squad started competing in rib cook-offs across the country. To date, they've won the best-ribs prize at the Twin Cities Ribfest four times. Ross and his wife have also come up with a recipe for a sweetly hot sauce that is "spicy for the connoisseur, yet mild enough for the whole family." It's tomato based, sweetened with Minnesota honey and brown sugar, and seasoned with Tabasco, chili powder, Worcestershire, liquid smoke, and lemon juice. "There's no recipe for ribs," Ross says. "It's all temperature and feel, and throwing some spice on them. Every set of ribs is different. There are only two racks of ribs on every pig, and every time it's a brand-new set of raw materials."

Roscoe's Favorite Ribs

1 slab pork spareribs
Lawry's seasoned salt
Kosher salt
Roscoe's Arousing Rib Rub

> Salt
>
> Sugar
>
> Garlic
>
> MSG
>
> Black pepper
>
> Onion powder
>
> Paprika
>
> Red bell pepper granules
>
> Oregano
>
> Liquid smoke

Sprinkle ribs with a mixture of Lawry's seasoned salt and kosher salt. Place them on a rack in your smoker, with water on the bottom of the smoker for moisture. (Roscoe's uses an Ole Hickory smoker.) Cook for approximately 3 to 3 1/2 hours at 235 to 250 degrees. When the ribs come out of the smoker, sprinkle with Roscoe's Arousing Rib Rub. Steve Ross suggests you play around with the quantities for his Arousing Rib Rub until you find the blend you like.

While still hot, stack the ribs in a plastic food container. Even though they are off the heat, the ribs will continue to cook a bit longer in this container. Allow to cool, and then cook them again at a temperature of 160 degrees, until warm, for about 10 to 20 minutes. Add a sweet and spicy barbecue sauce just before serving.

GENERAL COOKIN' TIP

★ Ross is a staunch believer that ribs should be cooked again after they're given time to cool: "It's my belief that the smoke has to set on a good smoked rib. I don't believe that a rib right out of the smoker is as good as a rib that has cooled down and then been brought back to temperature."

MIDWESTERN U.S. ★ ★ KILLER RIBS

SMOKY JON'S #1 BBQ

MADISON, WISCONSIN

According to Jon Olson, pictured above and known to friends, family, and barbecue lovers in Madison, Wisconsin, as Smoky Jon, "Good barbecue is where you find it, not where it's from."

And he's earned his right to an opinion: Smoky Jon has a lifetime of experience cooking barbecue. He grew up in a family whose business was meat and restaurants, and he started helping his dad at the age of ten, making family meals by cooking over wood and charcoal.

Olson feel particularly lucky to be making a living doing something he really loves. One reason that he's so passionate about barbecue is because he believes "it's truly something that we own—a real American cuisine." Olson went out on the competition circuit to

"show the world I had great sauce and great barbecue," he says. After twenty-four years and forty national and international awards, he has the trophies—on display in Smoky Jon's Wisconsin log cabin dining room—to back up his claims. For the past few years, due to the outcry from loyal customers, however, Olson has been staying close to home.

At Smoky Jon's, all the product is prepared in a wood-burning pit over Wisconsin shag hickory, using low heat, high humidity, and high smoke. "Barbecue is not for the impatient," says Olson. "The lower the heat, more tender the meat. 'Cue is one of the very best things to eat when it's done right and one of the worst when it's not done right."

Smoky Jon's Simple and Delicious BBQ Rib Recipe

This recipe is designed for novices. It's also great for winter, when it's too cold to cook outside.

Season your preferred meaty ribs with your favorite blend of seasonings, and let them sit for 1 hour. Preheat your oven to 325 degrees. Place the ribs in 1½ inches of warm water in a full-length pan. Cover the pan tightly with foil and cook the ribs until tender, approximately 2 hours. Remove the pan from the oven, drain it, and place the ribs in your freezer or refrigerator until they're completely cool.

Once the ribs are cool, grill them over medium-hot coals for 6 to 10 minutes on each side. Move the ribs to low, indirect heat, apply a generous coat of barbecue sauce, and allow it to sit for 10 minutes to glaze and penetrate the meat. Serve and enjoy!

GENERAL COOKIN' TIPS

★ Purchase the highest butcher-quality meat: "Good ribs aren't cheap and cheap ribs aren't good."

★ Smoky Jon's sauce is full-bodied and tomato based, and a combination of spicy and sweet. An ideal sauce, Olson says, will cause a "flavor explosion when you put it in your mouth." You want it to be spicy, but not so hot that you have to take a sip of water to cool your mouth between bites.

★ The key to good sauce are the spices: Olson uses different types of sweet and hot peppers, herbs and seasonings, lots of dry spice, and freshly diced natural white onion instead of granulated or powdered onion. "Anyone can make something hot," he says. "It's getting that curve, that balanced flavor," that makes a truly tasty sauce.

TWIN ANCHORS RESTAURANT & TAVERN

CHICAGO, ILLINOIS

This is a famous joint with a legendary past. The building dates back to 1881, and it was a tavern in the early 1900s and a speakeasy during Prohibition. Since 1932, though, it's been a great place for incredible ribs. Beginning in the 1950s, Frank Sinatra and his famous associates made a habit of dropping by to indulge in rack after rack of the popular barbecue delights. Legend has it that one night, Sinatra and friends ate their way through eighty racks.

The original owners, the Walters family, were members of the Chicago Yacht Club and gave the place its nautical name and its reputation for ribs. The current owners, the Tuzis, bought the restaurant in 1978. "My dad was an insurance agent—the only background he had with ribs was eating them," says Paul Tuzi. "But he was ready for a career change." Paul, along with his wife, Leslie, his sisters Mary Kay and Gina, and his brother-in-law Christian, took over the family business after his parents passed away.

Twin Anchors doesn't rest on its laurels: It remains one of the most popular places for ribs in Chicago. These days, diners wait up to two hours for a chance to taste the well-trimmed, slow-roasted baby backs at this historic Old Town landmark. And Sinatra's presence remains: Old Blue Eyes can be heard crooning nightly on the jukebox.

Slow-Roasted Ribs

1 rack baby back ribs
Salt
Paprika

Trim the membrane from the back of baby back ribs and remove excess fat—extra care in the prep makes for better-tasting ribs. Season the ribs with salt and paprika, and let them sit for 1 hour. Place the ribs in a baking pan, cook for 3 to 4 hours at 250 degrees, and then lower to 150 degrees and cook for another 3 hours. Meat should be very tender, but not shrink up on the bones. Finish on the grill with your choice of barbecue sauce.

GENERAL COOKIN' TIPS

★ Paul Tuzi used to be a judge in barbecue cook-offs in Chicago. Most of the contestants were weekend warriors who were very passionate about their cooking, but didn't prepare food for a living. "It was interesting to see what people came up with—things like blueberry sauce. Some good, some not so good," Tuzi said. But it's always good to experiment and try new things.

★ One unusual ingredient in Twin Anchors's secret sauce is pineapple juice. The sauce is sweet and tangy, but not too hot. "There are so many different possible approaches," Tuzi said. "You can really spice it up and make something heavily seasoned. We try to strike a balance with our tomato paste–based sauce."

★ Only season with rub, no sauce. Allow meat to cool before adding sauce and finishing on the grill—sauce tends to burn or become gloppy if cooked too long.

MIDWESTERN U.S. ★ ★ KILLER RIBS

THE SMOKE DADDY

CHICAGO, ILLINOIS

Doug Dunlay, co-owner of The Smoke Daddy, grew up in Kansas City and was immersed in barbecue culture from a young age. Now he's brought his barbecue expertise to the Windy City. Although Chicago—an "ethnically diverse town," with great food from different cultures—hasn't exactly been a "barbecue hotbed," according to Dunlay, barbecue culture is "starting to grow and take on a life of its own." The Smoke Daddy originally opened in 1994, and Dunlay and his cousin Mike took over in 2002.

"We have a great pipeline here for really great meat," says Dunlay. In Chicago, they let that excellent meat speak for itself. "We don't use as much rub. We accent it with a nice sauce, but don't oversauce or overspice." The meat isn't the only thing that's smokin'.

The Smoke Daddy hosts live blues and jazz seven nights a week, while the venue sets the scene: Housed in a narrow pink building with a neon "Smoke Daddy" sign and a glass-brick front, and red vinyl booths, the walls are plastered with photos of Chicago blues legends.

Chef Josh Rutherford smokes all ribs in the authentic pit they've affectionately named Lil' Red Smoker. "We sauce the meat after it's smoked and then flash it on the grill," says Dunlay. The Smoke Daddy serves up spareribs, baby backs, and rib tips, and offers three different types of sauces: Original, a vinegar-and-ketchup-based sauce with lots of cayenne, celery, pepper, and honey; Mustard Barbecue, which is also great on pulled pork; and a thicker tomato-based sauce called Sweet and Smoky.

The Smoke Daddy Mojo Rib Rub

$\frac{1}{2}$ **cup Spanish paprika**

1 tablespoon chili powder

2 tablespoons cayenne pepper

$\frac{1}{4}$ **cup black pepper**

1 tablespoon smoked paprika

1 tablespoon packed brown sugar

2 tablespoons oregano

2 tablespoons thyme

$\frac{1}{3}$ **cup kosher salt**

$\frac{1}{4}$ **cup garlic powder**

Mix all ingredients in a large bowl, then store in an airtight container until you want to use it. Sprinkle the ribs lightly at least 3 to 4 hours prior to smoking to allow the seasoning to fully enhance the meat. This rub will flavor 8 to 12 racks of ribs.

GENERAL COOKIN' TIPS

★ Don't use too much rub or sauce—you don't want either to overpower the flavor of the meat.

★ Smoke over hickory, apple, and cherry woods for about 6 hours at 220 to 225 degrees.

HICKORY PARK

AMES, IOWA

Owner David Wheelock is a modest man. In spite of the lines out the door of Hickory Park, the 425 seats that are divided into five dining rooms and are always filled, and the 3,500 pounds of pork ribs and 2,000 pounds of beef ribs they go through each week, he still (sincerely) insists he isn't doing anything special. Wheelock also insists that he is not a chef: "I learned how to make ribs by doing it."

There's an old-time feel to Hickory Park with elements dating back to before the restaurant's origins in 1970: an old-fashioned ice cream counter/soda fountain where they turn out ice cream sundaes, malts, and floats, as well as tin advertising signs, antique glass, metal ceilings, and church pew benches. But there are no padded banquettes at Hickory Park. "We don't want people to get too relaxed," Wheelock explains, because there are always more people waiting to be seated.

As the name of the place suggests, the beef and pork ribs are cooked over hickory wood. "It's what we're used to," he says. Other woods, like the fruit-wood favored by some pit masters, are hard to come by in Iowa. At Hickory Park, they keep four Southern Pride smokers busy, cooking ribs and other 'cue. The ribs aren't sauced until they've been removed from the smoker and cooled down. Then, they're doused in sauce and finished in the broiler just before serving.

Hickory Park Ribs

Marinade

    1 part white vinegar

    1 part red vinegar

    1 part soy sauce

    1 part Worcestershire sauce

    1 part teriyaki sauce

    $1/4$ part lemon juice

2 slabs baby back ribs

Water to cover ribs

Combine all ingredients except water, and pour the mixture over the ribs in a pan. Add water to cover the ribs, and refrigerate overnight for up to 24 hours. Allow the ribs to return to room temperature and smoke them for 2 to 3 hours at 200 degrees on your smoker.

Glaze

    $1/3$ cup smoky barbecue sauce

    $1/3$ cup sweet barbecue sauce

    $1/3$ cup orange juice

Combine equal parts of each ingredient and stir until well blended. You can substitute the orange juice with any sweet fruit juice, such as mango, pineapple, or apple. Once you remove the ribs from your smoker, lightly brush them with the glaze and place them on your grill. Heat the meat until the sauce is just caramelized, and the ribs are covered with a thin glaze. Remove and serve.

GENERAL COOKIN' TIPS

★ Don't be discouraged from smoking ribs at home. According to Wheelock, "some of these small home smokers do a better job than the big smokers" and are more efficient at infusing the meat with smoke flavor.

★ Be sure to buy good quality meat—you can taste the difference.

MIDWESTERN U.S. ★ KILLER RIBS

UNCLE EARNIE'S BEER, BAIT, AND BBQ

CEDAR CREEK, NEBRASKA

John Earnest, Uncle Earnie to those in the know, is a native of Nebraska, but he learned his 'cue in Memphis, Tennessee. The Shamrock Ham Hocks, a Memphis in May team, let him join their team, but they weren't going to let a Yankee contribute too much to smoking their ribs, particularly during a competition. Twelve trophies later, after cooking up everything from steak to lobster, and consistently winning, Earnest's teammates finally let him cook barbecue, too. When he returned to Nebraska, Earnest put his colorful Memphis knowledge to work, first cooking at parties and then finding a place on Highway 75 he thought would make a good roadside barbecue joint.

Uncle Earnie has made a name for Nebraska barbecue for ten years, and he's never stopped competing—in fact, he has seventeen smokers that he uses for competitions. He's won Best of Nebraska seven out of nine years, a Grand Champion World Pork Expo title in 2001, took fourth place at the 1998 Jack Daniel's World Championship, and eight state titles in the Kansas City BBQ Society.

This unique beer-bait-and-barbecue spot finishes the ribs off with a sweet and spicy sauce. The sauces come in spicy and mild, and Uncle Earnie is working on a hickory-smoked sauce that's due out soon. Plus, he uses a base of ketchup and chili sauce, and adds honey, hot peppers, garlic, and other spices to make his Kansas City wet sauce. Many of his customers like to order their ribs half and half—one-half wet (dipped in sauce) and one-half dry—for the perfect meal.

The Prestigious Barbecue Society Rib Rub

There are a lot of different combinations that make a good rub, according to Uncle Earnie. He recommends this recipe from the Greater Omaha Barbecue Society, of which he is a proud member.

2 tablespoons paprika

2 tablespoons chili powder

1 teaspoon cayenne pepper

2 tablespoons coarsely ground black pepper

2 tablespoons garlic powder

1$\frac{1}{4}$ teaspoon celery salt

$\frac{1}{2}$ teaspoon dry mustard

$\frac{1}{2}$ teaspoon sugar (optional)

Mix all the ingredients together, and store in an airtight container. This rub will flavor 2 racks of ribs. Sprinkle the dry rub generously all over the rack and let it sit for a few hours, or overnight if possible.

GENERAL COOKIN' TIPS

★ Uncle Earnie begins by cooking over hickory coals, making sure the hickory wood cooks down nicely with "a nice, sweet, mild smoke." Use apple wood during cooking, and finish with cherry wood for a "nice, sweet aroma."

★ He likes to smoke baby backs at 275 degrees for 3 to 5 hours, or until done, while spareribs need to stay in longer. You can tell they're done when the bone pulls back about half an inch, or if the rack bends when you pick it up with tongs.

OKLAHOMA JOE'S BARBECUE

KANSAS CITY, KANSAS

Jeff Stehney's barbecue joint in Kansas City may not be as well known as Arthur Bryant's or Gates, but he comes by his barbecue credentials authentically. His original partner was "Oklahoma Joe" himself, a.k.a. Joe Davidson, the owner and builder of a company that built and sold championship-quality wood- and coal-burning smokers, considered by many to be the best barbecue pits in the world. As top cooks on the competition circuit, Stehney and Davidson met and became friends, and in 1995, opened their first joint venture, Oklahoma Joe's, in Stillwater, Oklahoma. Davidson sold his interest in both the smoker company and they have since closed the Oklahoma restaurant, but Stehney went on to develop an excellent reputation in one of the capital cities of barbecue. The original Kansas City Oklahoma Joe's is a gas station, convenience store, liquor store, and barbecue joint all in one. When Stehney started out, he just rented the kitchen for catering. Now he owns the whole building, and the liquor store will soon make way for additional space for catering.

Until a few years ago, Stehney and friends competed under the name of Slaughterhouse Five, a punning reference to Kurt Vonnegut's novel. The team won eight Grand Championships, including the American Royal BBQ, three Reserve Grand Championships, and the Kansas City Barbeque Society's Grand Champion "Team of the Year" title. Their trophies and photographs of cookouts and competitions are now so abundant they fill not just one, but two locations.

Oklahoma Joe's Tasty Ribs

Dry rub

   4 tablespoons salt

   4 tablespoons granulated sugar

   2 tablespoons brown sugar

   1 tablespoon chili powder

   1 tablespoon paprika

   1 tablespoon cumin

   1 tablespoon MSG

   1 tablespoon granulated garlic

   2 tablespoons granulated onion

   2 tablespoons black pepper

   2 tablespoons white pepper

4 tablespoons brown sugar

3 slabs, loin back or spare pork ribs

8 ounces apple juice

Your favorite barbecue sauce

Preheat your grill or smoker to 250 degrees. Combine all the dry rub ingredients, but put one tablespoon of it in a separate bowl. Mix this tablespoon of dry rub with the 4 additional tablespoons of brown sugar. Demembrane the ribs and season both sides of the ribs with the dry rub. Place the ribs on your grill or smoker, away from direct heat. Add wood chunks to the fire and maintain a 250- to 275-degree fire. After 1½ hours, spray the ribs with apple juice, and spray again after 3 hours and remove them from the heat. Add the rub-and-brown-sugar mixture to the meat side of the ribs and wrap them in aluminum foil. Return the ribs to your grill or smoker and cook for another 1½ hours at 275 degrees. Remove the ribs from the foil, brush them with your barbecue sauce, and put them back on the grill or smoker for no more than 5 minutes. Remove the ribs and let them sit for 15 minutes before cutting.

GENERAL COOKIN' TIP

★ Oklahoma Joe's glaze their ribs with a sweetly hot sauce that's thick with tomato puree and ketchup, sweet from brown sugar, and spicy from a variety of spices.

GATES BAR-B-Q

─── KANSAS CITY, MISSOURI ───

Ollie Gates is a living legend—you can't talk about Kansas City ribs without discussing Gates Bar-B-Q. The Gates family got started back in 1946 when they took over a barbecue restaurant called O'Johnny's Ol' Kentucky Bar-B-Q. The pit master of the Ol' Kentucky, Arthur Pinkard, taught George Gates, a former railroad worker, and his son Ollie, the difference between backyard grilling and real, traditional smoked meat. While there were others making 'cue back then, a barbecue joint in the 1940s tended to be just a "shack by the track." Now there are about a hundred, and, thanks in part to Ollie Gates, Kansas City ribs are officially on the map.

Though the Kansas City style is often described as ribs slathered with a sweet, sticky sauce, the Gates family's tomato-based sauce is tangy, but it isn't too sweet or too sticky. "It's hot, but not too hot," explains Gates. But what really distinguishes the Kansas City cooking style, Gates says, is that in Kansas City they cook the meat directly over a fire in closed pits, which retain all the heat and smoke that infuses the ribs with savory flavor. Most important, Gates Bar-B-Q brings their unique style that has been tried and tested for over fifty years—a sure sign that Arthur Pinkard taught his protégées well.

Gates Rib Seasoning

1 cup sugar
$\frac{1}{2}$ cup salt
2 tablespoons paprika
2 tablespoons red pepper

In a medium bowl, mix all the ingredients together, and store in a tightly sealed jar. This seasoning will flavor several servings of ribs. When you're ready to cook, sprinkle pork spareribs with the rib seasoning, making sure both sides are covered evenly, but don't rub it into meat. Shake off any excess, and let the ribs stand in the seasoning until it starts to liquefy (approximately 15 minutes). There is no need to baste the spareribs—the seasoning does it all for you.

GENERAL COOKIN' TIPS

★ At Gates they only use pork spareribs. "Baby backs are a Johnny-come-lately," says Ollie. For the best cut, trim the end skin off the skirt, the extra meat along the bottom edge of the bone side, until all the excess fat is removed. Trim off the back, upper portion until the rib is properly contoured. You can also score the skirt between the bones to ensure the tenderness of the rib.

★ To cook, place the spareribs with the skirt down on a clean grate over an open fire. The Gates family recommends hickory chips and oak wood to add flavor to the smoke and direct fire, and make sure the temperature gets up to 230 to 250 degrees. Leave the ribs over the fire until they start to brown. Turn them over and move them to a low-temperature area on the grate, browning evenly on both sides.

★ The ribs are done when they are beautifully browned on both sides, and will lay limp over a cooking fork. Now you are ready to eat!

MIDWESTERN U.S.

KILLER RIBS

ARTHUR BRYANT'S BARBECUE

KANSAS CITY, MISSOURI

When Gary Berbiglia and his business partner Bill Rauschelbach took over Arthur Bryant's Barbecue after the death of its founder in 1982, they had big shoes to fill. Arthur Bryant's was a Kansas City legend, visited by Presidents Truman and Carter, actors such as Robert Redford and Jack Nicholson, and proclaimed "the single best restaurant in the world" by renowned writer Calvin Trillin. Berbiglia remembers stopping in at Arthur Bryant's for barbecue during his younger years while on the way home from ball games with his father and uncle. There was always an air of magic around Arthur Bryant's—part of the mystique focused on the sauce that Bryant mixed in five-gallon glass jars, one of which is still on display at the original location.

It's not easy capturing that sort of charm and standing out among the celebrated barbecuers in Kansas City. It's a large 'cue city, says Berbiglia, and people have a choice of eighty to a hundred barbecue joints, most of which turn out quality dishes, using high-quality meat that everyone gets from the same source. What sets a place apart is their cooking technique and sauce, and Arthur Bryant's original sauce is unusual for Kansas City. It's heavy on vinegar like a North Carolina sauce and light on tomatoes, and it's the heavy paprika base that gives this sauce its red color and "gritty" texture. Though they also stick with the basics, Berbiglia has come up with two new sauces: Rich and Spicy, a thick, tomato-based sauce with a variety of spices, and Sweet Heat, a tomato-based sauce with a honey-mustard flavor spiked with cayenne.

Arthur Bryant's Rib Rub

This rub is good on any type of pork, particularly baby backs and spareribs.

1 cup salt
$2/3$ cup paprika
$2/3$ cup sugar
$2/3$ cup packed brown sugar
1 tablespoon ground mustard
2 teaspoons white pepper (or black pepper)
$3/4$ teaspoon ground celery seed
2 teaspoons granulated onion
2 teaspoons granulated garlic

This recipe flavors 12 slabs of ribs. Mix all the ingredients together. Generously sprinkle both sides of the ribs with the rub and massage it in. Let them sit for at least 12 hours before cooking.

GENERAL COOKIN' TIPS

★ Buy ribs without membranes or ask your butcher to remove them, if possible.

★ Place the ribs over indirect heat with direct smoke, and cook at 225 degrees for about $4\frac{1}{2}$ to 5 hours. At Arthur Bryant's, they use a mixture of hickory and oak woods in their smoker.

★ When the ribs are almost ready, pull them out of the pit and dip the ribs, while still hot, in a sauce wash, a mixture that is 50 percent sauce and 50 percent water. This light coating of sauce seals in the juices, and keeps the ribs moist, explains Berbiglia.

MIDWESTERN U.S. ★ ★ KILLER RIBS

BUFFALO BOB'S SMOKEHOUSE

LAWRENCE, KANSAS

Though it's only forty miles west of Kansas City, Buffalo Bob's Smokehouse is far enough away that owner Bob Schumm can do his own thing, and he's been doing it since 1977. Schumm traces his interest in barbecue back to his days as a Boy Scout where he liked to cook outside, experimenting with the flavors of different woods (hickory is his favorite), seasonings, and spices. He honed his skills later on in life by experimenting with different ovens and pits, and eating at all the notable barbecue restaurants in his neck of the woods. Though Schumm acknowledges that "there are as many different types of barbecue as there are states in the union," he just makes his ribs the way he likes them. Buffalo Bob's offers three kinds: loin or baby back ribs, St. Louis cut, and the traditional sparerib, all served with homemade sauces.

Schumm believes that one reason for the growing interest in barbecue is because people are interested in "trying to find different ways to enjoy eating," evidenced by the increasing number of ethnic restaurants in Lawrence. What people really like, he says, is variety, and this diversity also shapes Schumm's clientele. The atmosphere at Buffalo Bob's is rustic, casual, and comfortable for people from all walks of life. "We get people in here in everything from overalls to suits. We've served six-week-old babies and elderly people with walkers. You're likely to see a workman sitting next to the chancellor of the University of Kansas—barbecue cuts across all boundaries."

Buffalo Bob's Fantastic BBQ Back Ribs

These meaty loin back (also known as baby back) ribs are smoked with a coating of dark red barbecue sauce, then slow cooked in a hickory smoker. Like many of the best sauces, the recipe is a secret and we've guessed at the proportions, but you should vary them to taste.

Barbecue sauce

> **1 cup ketchup**
> **$\frac{1}{4}$ cup packed brown sugar**
> **1 tablespoon red pepper flakes**
> **1 tablespoon finely ground black pepper**
> **2 tablespoons Worcestershire sauce**
> **1 tablespoon liquid smoke**
> **4 cloves garlic, minced**
> **2 tablespoons molasses**

$1\frac{3}{4}$- to 2-pound slab baby back ribs

Combine all the ingredients for the sauce and heat them in a saucepan on high heat, just until it boils. Lower the heat, stir, and simmer for 30 minutes.

Dip the ribs in the barbecue sauce and place them on a grate in the barbecue smoker oven at 270 to 295 degrees for 4 to 5 hours. The key to success is an authentic, home-built hickory wood smoker/oven and a huge open-water tank in the smoker to provide moist heat and prevent the meat from drying out.

GENERAL COOKIN' TIP

★ You want to cook the meat completely with heat generated from burning wood or wood burned down to charcoal in a 100 percent smoke-driven oven or barbecue pit, but keep in mind that green wood produces more smoke.

SOUTHERN U.S.
KILLER RIBS

DIXIE BONES

WOODBRIDGE, VIRGINIA

Even when he was in the real estate business, Nelson Head, owner and founder of Dixie Bones, dreamed of owning a real Southern barbecue house. His first major venture, located on Capitol Hill in Washington, D.C., attracted a prestigious political clientele, who enjoyed the Southern 'cue. Then he moved to Virginia, where the new location is "ugly on the outside," he says, "so we look like a real barbecue house." It's nice and comfortable inside, though, with eight booths and six tables. Photographs of Head's grandfather hunting or at work in his grocery store, as well as 1950s knick-knacks and memorabilia that Head collected when he was in the navy, adorn the walls. These decorations started a trend, and customers, particularly local Pentagon employees and police officers in training programs at the nearby FBI Academy, started contributing their own near-and-dear items—military patches, police badges, and other military souvenirs that their spouses wouldn't let them keep at home anymore.

For his smokin' ribs, Head orders the best-quality meat, has it custom-trimmed into very meaty St. Louis-cut racks, and smokes it over hickory wood for two to four hours, depending on the thickness of the rib. But he truly believes that the most important quality of a true Southern restaurant is the delectable, homemade side dishes, including collard greens, maca-roni and cheese, coleslaw made from garden-fresh cabbage, house-made rolls, and four or five pies. And of course, in true Southern style, everything they serve is made fresh from scratch everyday.

Mrs. Head's Spareribs

This is Nelson Head's mother's—Mrs. Jane Hill Head of Birmingham, Alabama—recipe for spareribs, and it's the foundation for the ribs they serve at the restaurant.

Dry rub

    1 teaspoon salt

    $1/4$ teaspoon packed dark brown sugar

    $1/8$ teaspoon turmeric

    $1/8$ teaspoon paprika

    $1/8$ teaspoon celery salt

    $1/8$ teaspoon black pepper

Combine all the ingredients, sprinkle over 4 to 5 pounds (2 racks) of St. Louis–cut spareribs, and let the meat sit in the refrigerator for 1 hour.

Marinade

    1 cup ketchup

    $3/4$ cup water

    $1/2$ cup chopped green pepper

    $1/2$ cup minced onion

    $1 1/2$ teaspoons minced fresh garlic

    $1/3$ cup cider vinegar

    $1/4$ cup packed dark brown sugar

    1 tablespoon Worcestershire sauce

    1 teaspoon dry mustard

    $1/2$ teaspoon Tabasco sauce

    $1/2$ teaspoon salt

    $1/4$ teaspoon dry basil

    $1/4$ teaspoon black pepper

Combine all the ingredients. Pour the marinade over the dry-rubbed ribs, cover, and refrigerate overnight. Cook in a slow smoker with hickory chips for 4 to 6 hours or until the ribs are tender and the fat next to the bones has liquefied. Serve without sauce!

MOONLITE BAR-B-Q INN

OWENSBORO, KENTUCKY

Catherine Bosley, the matriarch of the family that operates Moonlite Bar-B-Q, always liked to have a contingency plan. Together with her husband, Hugh, she bought a thirty-seat barbecue restaurant in 1963 and named it Moonlite. In order to pay for it, the couple sold their house and moved with their five children into her mother's house, and Catherine, a foreman at a local distillery, kept her day job, just in case. Today, the restaurant seats 350 and has more than 120 employees, including 25 family members.

At Moonlite, they barbecue all kinds of meat— chicken, beef, pork, and ribs—but their specialty is mutton, sheep that's at least a year old and tougher than lamb, with a gamier flavor. Welsh settlers popularized mutton in Owensboro and it's still popular at Moonlite— they serve 10,000 pounds a week!

The Bosleys cook mutton shoulder and ribs for twelve hours on their custom-built pit over hickory fire until it's tender, basting it while it cooks with their special vinegar dip. According to Catherine's grandson Patrick Bosley, mutton ribs don't have a lot of meat on them, and they're boney and fatty, but they're crispy on the outside, with tender meat near the bone, and "they have a whole lot of flavor." Toward the end of Catherine's life—she died in 2003 at the age of eighty-three—she finally allowed that Moonlite just might make it, but she advised Patrick to keep his options open, just in case.

Moonlite Bar-B-Q Mutton Ribs

Cooking Dip

    3 cups vinegar

    2 cups Worcestershire

    2 tablespoons Real Lemon® lemon juice

    5 cups water

    2 teaspoons black pepper

    $1\frac{1}{2}$ cups salt

Moonlite's Mutton Dip

    4 cups water

    $2\frac{1}{2}$ cups Worcestershire sauce

    2 teaspoons black pepper

    2 tablespoons packed brown sugar

    $\frac{1}{4}$ teaspoon MSG

    $\frac{1}{4}$ teaspoon allspice

    $\frac{1}{4}$ teaspoon onion salt

    $\frac{1}{4}$ teaspoon garlic, chopped

    2 teaspoons salt

    2 teaspoons Real Lemon

    $2\frac{1}{2}$ cups vinegar

2 racks of mutton ribs

Salt and pepper

Mix all ingredients for the Cooking Dip and cook the mixture just until it boils. Moonlite uses this versatile liquid to baste the meat while cooking to impart moisture.

Mix all ingredients for the Mutton Dip and cook just until it boils. Rub the top of the mutton with salt and pepper, and cook at 275 degrees for 4 hours over hickory fire, then turn the meat over and cook for 4 more hours. While cooking, baste with the Cooking Dip about every 1 to 2 hours. Serve with Moonlite Mutton Dip.

THE ORIGINAL Q SHACK

DURHAM, NORTH CAROLINA

The word "barbecue" in North Carolina is usually synonymous with pulled pork sandwiches and a vinegar-based sauce, but Q Shack chef Daniel Ferguson, a classically trained chef, isn't from North Carolina. So when he applied his training and palate to barbecue, he used the method he learned growing up to do it the way he liked best—Texas style.

The Original Q Shack combines some of the best elements of down-and-dirty 'cue with the best of up-scale barbecue with its traditional, down-home counter service paired with a sleek, contemporary feel. The picnic tables—indoors and outside on a large patio— are topped with industrial-chic galvanized steel sheets installed by Ferguson's dad. There's no wait staff and diners watch the meat being sliced to order.

As far as Ferguson could tell before he started making his delicious dishes, there wasn't any Texas 'cue in North Carolina. And even though Texas has an out-of-state reputation for beef barbecue, pork ribs are still a mainstay of Texas "Q," according to Ferguson. His pork ribs are meaty and tender, yet firm. The meat doesn't fall off the bone—a rack of ribs should just begin to bend in the middle, he says, not fall apart. "That's braising," says the chef. "The first sign of an overcooked rib is when it's falling off the bone."

Almost "The Original Q Shack" Rib Rub

Ferguson uses twenty-three spices in his dry rub, but here's a simplified version for the home cook.

1 part black pepper
1 part granulated garlic
1 part cayenne pepper
3 parts paprika
3 parts salt
1 part white sugar
4 parts packed light brown sugar
1 part ground cumin
1 part ground coriander
1 part ground chipotle

Throw all the ingredients into a bowl and mix together, then rub gently onto pork ribs.

GENERAL COOKIN' TIPS

★ Cook St. Louis–cut pork ribs at 250 degrees for 3 to 3½ hours, until they bend, but don't break, when you pick up a rack in the middle.

★ Texans like mesquite flavor, but too much mesquite can make your ribs bitter. Ferguson uses a blend of 75 percent hickory and 25 percent mesquite.

★ Ferguson offers two kinds of sauce: "My Sauce," a Texas-style ketchup-based sauce made with vinegar, honey, molasses, brown sugar, and chipotle, and "His Sauce," a nod to the Western North Carolina style that's vinegar-based with chiles, garlic, and a touch of tomato.

ALLEN & SON

CHAPEL HILL, NORTH CAROLINA

Y ou can't help but feel you're experiencing true barbecue when you eat at Allen & Son, and it's most likely because of what's found out back in the shack that houses the pit. In true Carolina style, Keith Allen, pictured above, cooks on hickory charcoal that he makes himself from hickory wood. He begins splitting wood in the afternoon, and wakes at 3 a.m. the following day to build a fire. It takes about thirty minutes to an hour for the wood to turn into coals, and then he takes the hottest coals from underneath and shovels them onto the bottom of his pit. There's no question that this pit is the real thing: the only source of heat and smoke is the hickory. Allen likes this type of wood, which is found all over the South, because it holds heat well, makes good coals, and has a pleasant, smoky flavor.

On any given day, you'll find Allen out back in the shack checking on pork butts and the requisite ribs or barbecuing whole pigs, sliced down the middle. Allen's ribs are soft and tender, with a sweet and tangy sauce. But don't ask him about other barbecue joints; Allen has never been to any other place—he's not interested in how they do it. He makes it the way he knows best and doesn't intend to change it. Though his barbecue has been hailed all over the country, Allen isn't interested in participating in any cook-off competitions—he gets all the encouragement he needs from his countless satisfied customers.

Allen & Son Sweet and Tangy Sauce

We managed to squeeze out some of the secret ingredients in Allen's hot barbecue sauce and we've estimated the proportions. However you mix it, Allen believes that sauce is key: "It's just smoked meat until you add the sauce," he says. "You need sauce to make it barbecue."

**1 cup high-quality apple cider vinegar (It should smell like apples; don't use
   cider-flavored vinegar.)**
1 cup ketchup
$\frac{1}{2}$ cup molasses
$\frac{1}{2}$ cup packed brown sugar
2 tablespoons hot red pepper flakes
2 tablespoons garlic salt
1 tablespoon black pepper
Oil to bind ingredients

Combine all the ingredients, mix them together well. Heat just until bubbling, then simmer for 15 to 20 minutes. Serve warm with 4 to 6 racks of ribs.

GENERAL COOKIN' TIPS

★ Keith Allen is one of the few professional pit masters who will admit to boiling his ribs, but he's not ashamed of his technique. "Memphis doesn't agree with this, but it's the way I do it. Parboiling gets rid of the film on the ribs and tenderizes the meat." Then he wraps the ribs in foil and puts them on top of pork shoulders in the pit, smoking them for 4 to 5 hours.

★ Allen doesn't put seasoning on until after the meat is cooked. Seasoning works well on warm foods, he says, "but you can't cook seasoning on food and expect it to do anything. Cold meat doesn't absorb much flavor."

★ Dip ribs in sauce after they're cooked, while still warm. Allen gives his ribs a bath in sauce, letting them marinate after they're cooked so they'll absorb more. He lets them sit and then reheats the ribs just before serving.

SOUTHERN U.S.
KILLER RIBS

THE BARBECUE JOINT

CHAPEL HILL, NORTH CAROLINA

Damon Lapas and Jonathan Childres, co-owners of The Barbecue Joint, don't seem too troubled by tradition. Though their place looks like a classic 'cue joint, with counter service and booth seating, the food, with its surprising gourmet twists, is not exactly what you'd expect from a typical barbecue place. In addition to North Carolina classics like sweet pork spareribs, you'll also find duck confit salad and Brussels sprouts listed on The Barbecue Joint's blackboard menu. The menu changes frequently—"We just erase something when we run out of it," Lapas says.

Lapas grew up on pig pickin's where the whole hog was the center of attention, but rarely ate ribs. "By the time we got there, they'd usually run out," he explains. It's hard for The Barbecue Joint to keep ribs in the house too, even though they're making more than the one pair that comes with one hog. Lapas and Childres decidedly prefer spareribs, because they're meaty, flavorful, and not obscenely overpriced. Their smoker is neither a traditional wood-only pit, nor a huge, gas-started, wood-burning Ole Hickory like you'll see at modern establishments. Instead, they make their 'cue their own way: in a small Chinese smoker with hickory, pecan, and oak chips. The spareribs are tender yet firm, and they serve them with their distinctive sauce that's tangy with tomato and vinegar, hot with chiles and cayenne peppers, and sweet from molasses and honey.

The Barbecue Joint Spareribs

Dry rub

> 1 cup salt
>
> 1 cup sugar
>
> 1 tablespoon granulated garlic
>
> 1 tablespoon granulated onion
>
> 2 teaspoons celery seed
>
> $\frac{1}{2}$ cup paprika
>
> $\frac{1}{4}$ cup chili powder
>
> $\frac{1}{4}$ cup freshly ground black pepper
>
> 1 teaspoon lemon pepper
>
> 1 teaspoon rubbed sage
>
> 1 teaspoon thyme
>
> **Pinch cayenne**

Preheat grill to 300 degrees. Combine all the ingredients, and coat 2 racks of pork spareribs with the mixture. Cover the ribs and grill them low and slow over indirect coals for $2\frac{1}{2}$ to 3 hours. While the ribs are grilling, prepare the sauce.

Sauce

> 1 pint ketchup
>
> 1 pint cider vinegar
>
> $\frac{1}{3}$ cup honey
>
> $\frac{1}{4}$ cup molasses
>
> 1 tablespoon chile flakes
>
> 1 tablespoon cayenne
>
> 2 tablespoons salt
>
> $\frac{1}{4}$ cup Worcestershire sauce
>
> 1 tablespoon minced garlic
>
> 2 tablespoons black pepper

Combine all the ingredients and cook for 15 to 30 minutes over low heat, stirring occasionally. When the ribs are done, slice and coat them with sauce, and serve with additional sauce if desired.

COZY CORNER RESTAURANT

MEMPHIS, TENNESSEE

Cozy Corner is the perfect name for this family-run joint, but the owners didn't come up with that name; they just adopted the one that was already on the door. "My husband would hold a nickel until the eagle came off," Desiree Robinson said, referring to her late husband, Ray. " 'No way we're going to call it Ray's Barbecue if it would cost me money to change it,' " was his attitude, as she recalls it.

Before they opened Cozy Corner on "the same month and date that Elvis died," the couple did have a place called Ray's Barbecue, in Denver, Colorado, modeled after the flavors from Culpeppers, a now-defunct and once-renowned Memphis restaurant. The Robinsons experimented with various techniques and ingredients, and considered important issues, such as

whether to mop or not to mop. (They decided against mopping.) When they moved back home to Memphis, friends and family begged them to open a place in the Bluff City.

Twenty-eight years later, the ribs are still cooked on the Chicago-style pit left behind by the former tenant. They used to cook the ribs overnight, but now the cooking is done during in the day in full view of the customers, who are frequently drawn in by the smell of the smoke. The ribs are seasoned with salt and pepper, plus "some other things," and cooked over charcoal with a special sauce. How long they need to cook "depends on the size of the rib, heat, what else is on the pit, and who's cooking," says Robinson, pictured above with her daugher, Val, and her son, Ray Jr.

Desiree Robinson's Home-Cooked Pork Ribs

When cooking at home, Desiree Robinson recommends using an untrimmed rib, with the tip still on it, so there's plenty of meat for the whole family and nothing goes to waste.

1 slab ribs, uncut (approximately 2$^{3}/_{4}$ pounds)
$^{1}/_{2}$ teaspoon salt
$^{1}/_{2}$ teaspoon black pepper
$^{1}/_{2}$ teaspoon garlic salt
$^{1}/_{4}$ teaspoon McCormick's all-season salt
$^{1}/_{4}$ teaspoon Goya Adobo all-purpose seasoning
20 drops grenadine

Wash the rack of ribs with water and pat it dry. Spread out a double layer of foil, and place the rack on the foil and sprinkle it with the spices. Then, lightly drizzle the ribs with the grenadine syrup, across the entire top surface of the slab. Wrap the ribs tightly in foil and refrigerate for 24 hours. Remove when you're ready to cook, and preheat your oven to 375 degrees—make sure it's hot! Bake the ribs for 1$^{1}/_{4}$ hours, take the foil off the top, and let the slab brown in the oven for 15 minutes. Then, cut 'em and eat 'em.

GENERAL COOKIN' TIPS

★ You can tell when the ribs are done when they pull away a little from the tip of the bone, and you can see a fifth of an inch of the bone and a fork goes into the meat easily.

★ At Cozy Corner they prefer smaller ribs "from a young pig—not a piglet—but young and tender, with a delectable flavor."

SOUTHERN U.S. ★ KILLER RIBS ★

BIG BOB GIBSON BAR-B-QUE

DECATUR, ALABAMA

Big Bob Gibson was a railroad worker who started smoking barbecue in his Decatur, Alabama, backyard in 1925. Soon, the scent of aged hickory–smoked meat drew neighbors eager to buy his savory barbecue, and Big Bob settled into a permanent shop in the 1950s. All of Gibson's five children are passionate about barbecue too, and made it their lives' work. In the 1980s, the third generation, Gibson's grandson Don McLemore and his wife, Carolyn, took responsibility of the Decatur restaurant, but it didn't stop there.

The demand for 'cue grew exponentially, and soon the fourth generation was lured into the business when McLemore offered his son-in-law Chris Lilly a barbecue job. Luckily, Lilly took to barbecue like sauce on pork, training in the pits with Jerry Knighten, who was trained

by Big Bob himself. McLemore and Lilly have kept Big Bob Gibson's traditions going while also moving in new directions: Their pork ribs didn't even appear on the menu until the 1990s, but that didn't stop them from making up for lost time—they continue to cook up delectable ribs to this day.

Big Bob's also had their famous vinegar-and-mayonnaise-based sauce, but McLemore wasn't happy with the commercially produced red sauce they were serving, so he and Lilly created a traditional, sweet, tomato-based sauce. The sauce has twice won the Memphis in May World Championship Cook-Off and was named "Best Sauce on the Planet" out of more than 500 entries in the American Royal International Barbecue Sauce contest in 1998. Big Bob sure would be proud!

Pineapple-Marinated Loin Back Pork Ribs with Honey-Garlic Tomato Glaze

Honey-Garlic Tomato Glaze

- $\frac{1}{4}$ cup olive oil
- $\frac{1}{4}$ cup chopped onion
- 2 teaspoons minced fresh garlic
- 4 cups ketchup
- $1\frac{1}{3}$ cups packed dark brown sugar
- 1 cup vinegar
- 1 cup apple juice
- $\frac{1}{4}$ cup honey
- $1\frac{1}{2}$ tablespoons Worcestershire sauce
- $1\frac{1}{2}$ tablespoons liquid smoke
- 1 teaspoon salt
- 1 teaspoon black pepper
- 1 teaspoon cayenne pepper
- 1 teaspoon celery seed

6 slabs loin back ribs (12 large servings)
Dry rub marinade
$4\frac{1}{2}$ cups pineapple juice

Lightly sauté the onions and garlic with olive oil in a large saucepan. Pour in remaining glaze ingredients and heat until the sauce bubbles. Remove from heat and serve at room temperature. Preheat cooker to 250 degrees. Generously apply your favorite basic rub, with $4\frac{1}{2}$ cups of pineapple juice added, to the demembraned ribs. Place the ribs meat-side up in your smoker and cook for $2\frac{1}{4}$ hours. Remove them from the smoker and wrap each slab meat-side down in double aluminum foil, sealing tightly. Cook for 1 hour. Remove the wrapped ribs from the smoker and apply a light coat of rub to the meat side of the ribs. Place uncovered in the smoker, meat-side up, for 30 minutes. Remove the ribs from the smoker, and brush the glaze on both sides of the ribs. Place them back in the smoker for another 15 minutes until the sauce caramelizes.

THE SALT LICK

DRIFTWOOD, TEXAS

Scott Roberts traces the origins of his family's famous barbecue restaurant back to 1867, when his ancestors trekked across the country in covered wagons before they settled in Driftwood. Along the way, they seared and slow-cooked meat over a wood fire on metal grills supported by rocks. These pioneers carried with them a style of cooking and a set of recipes they would pass down for generations. Scott's father, Thurman Roberts, continued the barbecue tradition with a large, open barbecue pit that Scott helped build for him on the side of a road near their family ranch. "On Thursdays he would start cooking in the evening and sleep by the side of the road until he had sold out of meat," Scott recalls. Based on the

popularity of the food, Thurman and his wife, Hisako, decided to open The Salt Lick in 1968. Over the years the restaurant has grown a bit from a few picnic tables under the trees—they now have the capacity to seat eight-hundred people!

Both the pit and the building that houses the restaurant were crafted out of limestone that Roberts and his family quarried themselves on their ranch. "Our limestone pit re-creates the way they cooked on the wagon train, and, today, we still finish all our meats over the open pit," says Scott. Thurman Roberts passed away twenty-two years ago, but Scott's mother (who's now ninety-two) still checks up on the staff at The Salt Lick to make sure they're doing it right.

Salt Lick-Style Beef Ribs

Salt

Black pepper

Cayenne pepper

6- to 8-pound seven-bone rack of prime beef ribs

Your favorite barbecue sauce (made without tomatoes so the sauce doesn't
burn, and make sure the sauce is acidic with a high sugar content)

Mix the salt, black pepper, and cayenne pepper in proportions that you prefer, and liberally rub both sides of the meat with the mixture. Place the ribs over direct heat and sear them until the spices have set in and the meat is slightly caramelized. Remove them from direct heat and move to a part of the smoker that's about 225 degrees. Baste the ribs with barbecue sauce and turn them at least three times during the cooking process. Cook for 5 to 6 hours, or until the meat is falling off the bone.

GENERAL COOKIN' TIPS

★ Use oak wood, oak charcoal, or hickory pecan. Roberts avoids mesquite.

★ Demembrane your ribs by peeling the membrane off the back of the beef ribs before cooking.

SMITTY'S MARKET

LOCKHART, TEXAS

In the small town of Lockhart, Texas, population 13,000, there are four barbecue joints, and many consider Lockhart the "barbecue capital of the world." The town's history goes way back, especially in the case of Kreuz Market, the predecessor of Smitty's Market. The owners of Kreuz Market, established as a meat market in 1899, started selling smoked meat to locals by the pound, slicing it and wrapping it in butcher paper.

In 1948, Edgar "Smitty" Schmidt, an employee of the market, bought the business, housed in a redbrick building, from the Kreuz family, and kept their famous name. Schmidt's daughter, Nina Sells, renamed the original place Smitty's after her father when her brother opened a new place nearby, taking the Kreuz name with him. Now, Nina's son, John Fullilove, is the current pit master, and he continues to slice the meat onto butcher paper and sell it by the pound. In addition, Smitty's has a no-frills dining room with long wooden tables where you can eat it.

The cooking method hasn't changed much since 1900. They still don't use any electricity or gas, and customers stand in line right next to the fire when they order. Using a fire that never goes out—the pit is lit from coal left over from the day before—the ribs are smoked over post oak, a type of wood plentiful in the South. But, beware if you visit Smitty's: These extra-special ribs are served only on the weekends.

Smitty's Market Ribs

Fullilove's cooking method is simple, and until 2003, he didn't even put sauce on the ribs.

1 rack spareribs
Smitty's Seasoning
    Salt
    Dash black pepper
    Dash red pepper
Your favorite barbecue sauce

Cut the brisket bone off the sparerib or ask your butcher for St. Louis–cut ribs. Lightly season the ribs on both sides with Smitty's Seasoning and cook them at 350 to 400 degrees until both sides have a grilled appearance, about 2 hours. Once the ribs are cooked thoroughly, baste with your sauce of choice. Fullilove recommends a thick, sweet, tomato-based sauce, with mustard and sweet pickle juice that will stick to the ribs.

GENERAL COOKIN' TIPS

★ Buy good-quality meat and cook it fast. Fullilove prefers higher temperatures— 350 to 400 degrees—and cooks his ribs for about 2 hours. "If you buy good meat, you don't need to cook it that much," he said.

★ Keep your seasonings simple to let the wood smoke add flavor to the meat.

★ Use wood that's plentiful. "We use post oak because it grows around here like brush, but I say, wood is wood. Everyone says mesquite burns too hot, but it depends on how you burn it!"

★ To test if the meat is done, insert a toothpick or fork into the meat. It should feel like you're sticking it in a warm stick of butter.

BUBBALOU'S BODACIOUS BAR-B-QUE

— WINTER PARK, FLORIDA —

Sam Meiner likes to call himself the Big Pig. A former lawyer with a ferocious sense of humor, Meiner grew up in the restaurant business and couldn't wait to get back to it. In 1986, he opened the first Bubbalou's Bodacious Barbecue, and now he has five locations in Florida. Meiner has worked hard, and he is unambiguously proud that Bubbalou's was designated "America's Best BBQ Dive" by the Food Network.

Bubbalou's has a reputation for their barbecued meats, Southern food, and Killer BBQ Sauce, as well as their Psycho Sauce, which Meiner has dubbed "the hottest sauce on the planet." In the course of a year, they serve more than 150,000 pounds of spareribs and 75,000 pounds of succulent baby back ribs. They make the pork ribs with loving care, rubbing with a mixture of salt, garlic, onion, and black pepper, and basting every half hour with a mop of vinegar and water, plus some secret ingredients. The meat is then slow-smoked over oak, and finished with a tomato-based sauce that's sweetened with brown sugar.

For a really special treat, the Big Pig also offers up a unique Florida delicacy: barbecued alligator ribs. Though Meiner likes to kid, these ribs are no joke. Meiner and his wife have a license to hunt alligator in the Florida swamps—she gets a handbag and he gets gator ribs. It's an adventure for them, because, as Meiner says, "they're the only ribs that are likely to eat you before you can eat them."

"Eat or Be Eaten"
Bodacious Bar-B-Que Gator Ribs

Farm-raised alligators tend to be about 4 to 5 feet long with slabs of ribs that fit in your hand, while in the wild, they tend to be around 8 to 10 feet long with rib racks around the size of a letter-sized sheet of paper. Unless you hunt your own alligator, the ribs you buy will come frozen. This recipe serves 6 to 12 people

6 pounds alligator ribs (12 slabs)
1 cup table salt
Everglades seasoning (a regional mix of herbs and spices, with MSG)
Juice of 2 Florida oranges, limes, or lemons
6 whole Florida grapefruits
1 cup melted butter with a hefty dash of Tabasco sauce and lemon juice added
Barbecue sauce of your choice

Fire up grill with a high flame and defrost the ribs. Wet the ribs with water and coat them liberally with table salt, then rinse all the salt off with water once the meat is thoroughly coated. Place the ribs on a flat tray and squeeze fresh citrus juice liberally on the ribs. Sprinkle on Everglades seasoning and let the ribs sit for about 10 minutes.

When the fire is hot, cut each grapefruit in half and place the cut side up on the grill for 10 minutes until it just begins to steam, then put the ribs on the grill rack next to the grapefruit. Cook the ribs for about 3 to 4 minutes on one side, drizzling a little of the butter mixture on the meat before turning. Turn the ribs and repeat, making sure that both sides are seared—the ribs should now be lightly browned and the meat will be white. Either brush the ribs lightly with your favorite barbecue sauce and flame them once more, or remove them from the grill and squeeze on lemon juice and melted butter, then serve each slab with a grilled grapefruit half.

JONES BARBEQUE

SEATTLE, WASHINGTON

Jones Barbeque is truly a family business. "Everybody in the family has a specific job—even my mother bakes. My wife makes the cheesecakes, I make the pies, my son takes care of the meat, and my daughter runs around to the different restaurants as general manager," says patriarch William Jones about the division of labor that encourages peace in the family. But the family connection predates even the first outpost that Jones opened in Seattle in 1988. Jones gives the credit to his own father, a chef and waiter in Arkansas, who was known for his barbecue—he built barbecue pits out of empty refrigerators—and his amazing sauce. Eventually, his dad taught him to make his famous sauce: a blend of mustard, ketchup, garlic, brown sugar, white sugar, vinegar, and other secret

ingredients. The thick and sweet sauce that Jones's serves is based on his father's recipe, and comes in three versions: mild, medium with a little bite, and hot, which is spiked with hot sauce made from different peppers that'll "make you sweat."

Like many rib joints, Jones Barbeque attracts people from all walks of life with their brand of Southern hospitality: "Everybody comes: working people, all nationalities, all different people come to Jones Barbeque—senior citizens, everybody." Good barbecue, according to Jones, is made with good smoke, superior sauce, and a first-class rub. About his own 'cue, Jones says, "I could eat it all the time. I ain't going to get tired of the rub or the sauce—you can eat it anytime."

Jones Honey-Barbeque Sauce

2 cups packed brown sugar

$1/2$ cup chili powder

$1/2$ cup onion powder

1 teaspoon pepper

3 teaspoons salt

1 cup vinegar

1 cup Worcestershire sauce

6 cups ketchup

1 cup molasses

1 cup honey

$1/4$ cup liquid smoke

$1/2$ cup water

Combine all of the dry ingredients in a large bowl and stir thoroughly. Next, add the vinegar, Worcestershire sauce, and ketchup, mixing well after each addition. Carefully stir in the molasses, honey, and liquid smoke, until thoroughly combined. Pour the mixture into a medium saucepan and simmer for about 20 minutes, or until all ingredients have been well dissolved, adding water to the mixture as needed. Make sure your sauce is consistent—not too thick and not too thin. This sauce will cover about 12 racks of ribs.

GENERAL COOKIN' TIPS

★ Be sure to start with a good rib rub, and rub it into the meat really well. Jones Barbeque makes their rub with garlic, onion, meat tenderizer (a powder that helps break down protein), brown and white sugar, chili powder, and paprika, and uses it on both beef and pork ribs.

★ Slow-cook the ribs over wood smoke until they are nice and tender. "Figure out what's the best wood available in your area," Jones says, who uses cherry or alder. Smoke the rack for about 6 hours. You can tell it's done, he says, "when you lift the rack with tongs, and it bends in half and is about ready to fall apart."

WESTERN U.S. ★ ★ KILLER RIBS

WILLOW CREEK CAFÉ & SALOON

WILLOW CREEK, MONTANA

In a town with a population of 250, a restaurant that seats up to ninety people may seem like an extravagance, but this cafe regularly packs them in. Chef and owner Dean Mitchell says that he knows just about all the locals, and his partner and co-chef Tim Andrescik lives above the saloon. The place, an old Western-looking two-story building that dates back to around 1906, was in pretty good condition when they took it over in the late 1990s; they left the bullet holes in the original tin ceilings for an authentic feel.

But even if it weren't the only restaurant in the quiet town of Willow Creek, the two men would still draw folks from distant points with their honey-mustard baby backs. They started making the ribs as a special, but soon this delectable dish became the most popular item on the menu. The guest book is filled with testimonials from people all over the country who vow that these are the best ribs they've ever had—in spite of the fact that Mitchell and Andrescik don't smoke their baby backs.

"Meat that's smoked in a pit, that's smoked meat," says Mitchell, and he does his share of smoking: preparing smoked mushrooms to serve on pulled pork; smoked beef tri-tip for sandwiches; and chicken for their soups. But, "barbecue is something that's cooked on the grill," Mitchell asserts, flouting diehard barbecuing convention, and so Willow Creek Café's ribs are cooked in the oven and finished on the grill.

Honey-Mustard Ribs

Mitchell won't share the exact ingredients in his honey-mustard sauce ("it's a trade secret"), but people are always trying to figure out what's in it. "I'm tasting anise," a guest might say, and Mitchell will nod his head and say, "Might be a little bit of that in there."

Wash
- **½ cup brewed strong coffee**
- **1 teaspoon garlic**
- **½ teaspoon pepper**
- **½ teaspoon five-spice powder**
- **1 tablespoon mustard**
- **2 tablespoons vinegar**
- **Dash Frank's original Red Hot sauce**

1 rack baby back ribs

1 lemon

1 cup honey-mustard barbecue sauce (either store-bought or your own recipe)

Combine the ingredients to make the wash, adjusting the proportions to your taste, and dip the ribs in it. Place the ribs in a large pan and sprinkle them with the juice of one lemon. Bake them at 500 degrees for about 2½ hours. Remove the pan from the oven and place the ribs on the grill on direct heat for 10 minutes until brown, so the sauce carmelizes. Slather with additional honey-mustard barbecue sauce until glazed.

GENERAL COOKIN' TIPS

★ If you can make great ribs on the grill that you love, don't worry about what anyone else says!

★ A great honey-mustard sauce is a well-balanced blend of flavors in which no one flavor dominates the others. Experiment with different proportions, spices, and other seasonings to find your favorite combination.

ROAD HOUSE BBQ

EAGLE, IDAHO

Ross Tilbury knows quality meat. Before he brought his brand of Texas-style barbecue via Shreveport, Louisiana, to Idaho when he opened the Road House, he was in the meat business. So it's no surprise that he uses choice grade or better. Tilbury traces his barbecue style to Bodacious BBQ in East Texas. He competed in the Houston World Championship in 1993 and 1994 as an assistant on the Bodacious team, and learned how to build a fire, when the fire is right, and where to put the meat on the fire. "When you compete on a team, you learn to read the signs, like when it's telling you it's ready," Tilbury said.

In 1993, on a tip from a friend who had recently moved to Boise, Tilbury moved to the Gem State to fill the need for serious barbecue. Tilbury and his wife are equal cohorts in Road House BBQ. She helps prep side dishes, greets the customers, and works the counter, while Tilbury is the hands-on pit master. He believes it is part of his job to educate the locals who are accustomed to barbecue as an equivalent to hamburgers and hot dogs. "Barbecue is a large piece of meat smoked over a long period of time until it's tender," he tells the uninitiated. Road House BBQ is also the go-to caterer when bands come to town—they've provided the backstage vittles for Los Lobos, Nitty Gritty Dirt Band, and Robert Earl Keen, a singer-songwriter from Texas.

Road House Rub

1 tablespoon sugar
¹⁄₄ teaspoon black pepper
1 teaspoon garlic salt
¹⁄₈ teaspoon cayenne pepper
¹⁄₂ teaspoon paprika

Mix all the ingredients together and gently rub it into 1 slab of your preferred kind of meaty ribs. Feel free to use your favorite spices and seasonings to add extra flavor.

GENERAL COOKIN' TIPS

★ Use the best-quality meat you can get your hands on—it's worth the extra money when you are putting all that work and time into cooking it! Look for a heavy piece with good meat covering and no exposed bone.

★ After you rub the spice mixture into the meat, wrap the rack in cellophane and let it rest for about 1 hour. This step ensures that the meat will be tender.

★ Smoke for 3 or 4 hours. Tilbury prefers a little tug in the meat: "If the ribs fall off the bone, they're overcooked."

EAGLE RIB SHACK

EAGLE, IDAHO

The moment Andrew Petrehn opened the doors of Eagle Rib Shack, his first customer told him he was going to need a bigger place. It's funny, then, that Petrehn almost didn't even open this small rib shack. As a native of Kansas City, he always made killer KC ribs, and so his wife, Saundra, encouraged him to enter Boise's 2003 Thrill of the Grill Barbecue Contest. She included the following stakes: If he won the contest, he would open his own place, and if he lost, he would quit griping about the lack of KC 'cue in Idaho. To the surprise of many, Petrehn won the contest and a week later signed a lease on a former dairy outbuilding. Then he spent six months getting ready, developing recipes, and transforming the interior into a rustic tribute to the West with photographs of cattle drives and chuck wagons.

Petrehn incorporates a range of flavors that he discovered on his travels around the country as a pilot of hot-air balloons, and he makes different sauces to represent the country. The Texas sauce is spicy and sweet; Memphis is mustard based; Carolina is a spicy cider vinegar that's best on pulled pork; #7 is so called for its place on a scale of ten for spiciness (7 out of 10); and there are three Kansas City-style sauces—tomato-based, sticky, and sweet in mild, original, and hot. Petrehn encourages people to follow their own taste: "Find what you like, mix 'em, and don't pay attention to anyone else."

Smoked Lamb Spareribs with Herb Rub

1 rack lamb spareribs
Canola oil
Seasoning salt
4 tablespoons crushed, dried rosemary
4 tablespoons crushed, dried thyme
Barbecue sauce, for basting

Remove the membrane of the dry lamb spareribs using a paper towel. Lightly oil the ribs with canola oil, and then season with a great seasoning salt (try Magic Seasoning Salt). Encrust the ribs generously with the herbs. Using a combination of apple, hickory, and cherry woods, smoke at 200 degrees for 6 to 8 hours until the meat starts to pull away from the ribs. Baste with your favorite barbecue sauce during the last 30 minutes of cooking, and serve.

GENERAL COOKIN' TIPS

★ Petrehn uses various types of wood in his three smokers because each kind produces unique flavors and pairs well with different meats. There's no hickory in Idaho, so he brings it back from Missouri. He also uses fruitwoods such as apple and peach, as well as pecan, alder, and oak, from California.

★ Kansas City ribs are usually pork, but Petrehn doesn't limit his choice of meats. He smokes lean buffalo back ribs when he can get a good supply, Kobe-style beef back ribs from Idaho's Snake River Farms, pork baby back and spareribs, and tender lamb spareribs.

WESTERN U.S.
KILLER RIBS

Q4U

WEST VALLEY, UTAH

Q4U owners Tommy Sisna and his wife, Becci, dreamed of owning their own barbecue restaurant, but they wanted to make sure they knew what they were getting into first. So they spent some time serving up their 'cue at fairs and festivals. The idea of settling down with a restaurant was especially appealing to this couple, because they both grew up as "military brats" whose families were constantly relocating. T, as Tommy is known, developed his taste for barbecue living all over the country as a child and then a young musician on tour. T had some success as a musician, but cooking, and in particular barbecue, is his true calling.

After a successful year testing and experimenting their homemade tomato-based sauces, T and Becci opened a permanent restaurant in 1997. They participated in the Great Western Rib Fest in Reno, and in their second year in existence, they won second place. Even though they are located off the beaten path to the west of Salt Lake City, these diehard barbecue competitors have managed to maintain national recognition for their hands-on owner-operated barbecue joint. "When your peers give you the props about what you've done with an itty-bitty place," T said, "that's a great feeling!"

Lemon Ribs

This recipe can be used for basting when grilling over low coals, as a mop when smoking, or as a sauce when cooking in the oven.

Lemon sauce
- $1/2$ **cup water**
- **1 chicken-flavored bouillon cube**
- **1 cup pineapple juice**
- **3 tablespoons packed brown sugar**
- **2 cloves garlic, minced**
- $1/4$ **cup minced onion**
- $1/4$ **cup ketchup**
- $1/4$ **cup lemon juice**
- **2 tablespoons cornstarch**

Salt and pepper to taste
1 rack well-trimmed baby back or spareribs

Combine all the sauce ingredients in a saucepan, and season to taste with salt and pepper. Bring to a boil and stir well. Lower the heat, and simmer for about 5 minutes; then set aside.

If you're smoking the ribs, cook them bone-side down until done. If you're grilling, start with meat-side down until they're brown, then turn them meat side up. To cook in the oven, position the oven racks in the top and bottom thirds of the oven and preheat to 325 degrees. Sprinkle the ribs with salt and pepper, and wrap each rib rack tightly in foil, enclosing completely. Divide the foil packets between 2 baking sheets and bake until the ribs are very tender (about 2 hours total), switching positions of the baking sheets halfway through. Cool the ribs slightly in the foil, and pour off any fat. Once the ribs are cooked, heat the grill up to medium-low heat. Cut each rib rack into individual ribs, and set aside 1 cup of the sauce. Add the ribs to a bowl with the remaining sauce and toss to coat. Grill the ribs until brown and glazed, turning to prevent burning, for about a total of 5 minutes. Serve with sauce.

MEMPHIS MINNIE'S

SAN FRANCISCO, CALIFORNIA

Bob Kantor is a barbecue purist: he's a zealous supporter of the real slow-smoked techniques of Southern barbecue that he calls an "endangered species." With training at the California Culinary Academy, Kantor "quickly realized what barbecue was about," he says, "and it totally grabbed me." He read every book he could get his hands on, joined barbecue organizations, and traveled around the country for two years, visiting pits in Kansas City, Chicago, Texas, the Carolinas, and Mississippi.

Because "if it's cooked with gas it's not barbecue," Kantor is attached to his smokers, and he gives them all names. Olivia, for instance, hails from Texas and burns nothing but white oak, which is indigenous to the area. He also cautions against the overuse of sauce.

"Faux 'cue," he says, "is dependent on sauce for its flavor. The role of sauce is to obscure what real barbecue is about—the meat!" Memphis Minnie's—named in tribute to Kantor's mother, Minnie, who grew up in Memphis—offers four different sauces, served on the side and all kettle-made in house: a ketchup-based Texas red, a mustard-based South Carolina, and a vinegar-based North Carolina, plus a hot sauce. Kantor was "dragged kicking and screaming to produce a hot sauce," as he doesn't really feel there is a place for it on real barbecue ribs. But he created Beelzebub's Hot Sauce, a sauce so hot that he hoped no one would want to eat it, though fire-eaters are not deterred, drenching their meat, "until the smoke and flames are coming out of their ears and noses."

Memphis Minnie's Rib Rub

This rub works well with all cuts of pork.

2 parts salt

1 part granulated white sugar

1 part packed medium brown sugar

1 part black pepper

1 part granulated garlic

1 part Spanish paprika

Mix all ingredients and process in a food processor with a sharp blade for a finer consistency.

GENERAL COOKIN' TIPS

★ Use only fresh meats. The best barbecue cannot be made with meat that has been frozen.

★ Rubs and marinades are fine additions to "bring out" or "brighten" the natural flavors of the meat, but use them sparingly so as not to overwhelm the flavor of the meat, and, of course, true barbecue needs no sauce. "Sauce is good, but sauce does not make barbecue. No more than a beautiful woman is defined by jewels and clothes," says Kantor.

★ Ribs should be "skinned." The membrane acts as a barrier to absorption of smoke, and it's also "downright unpleasant" to eat, according to Kantor.

★ If there is a secret to cooking barbecue, it's that it must be cooked "low and slow." Grilling is the antithesis of Southern-style barbecue because great barbecue shouldn't be rushed.

MEMPHIS CHAMPIONSHIP BARBECUE

LAS VEGAS, NEVADA

For proof that champions are made, not born, you have only to look to Mike Mills and his Apple City Barbecue team. No one, not even Mills himself, expected a Yankee from Murphysboro, Illinois, to win the grand prize at the Memphis in May World Championship Barbecue Contest the first time he entered in 1990. But this win was no fluke; he went on to win a total of four World Championships and three Grand World Championships, a record that remains unbroken. The journey to Las Vegas began when a gentleman who had relocated there from Memphis was frustrated by the lack of good barbecue. He went

in search of the best barbecue, and found Mike Mills. They started in 1994 with one eatery out by the air force base in Las Vegas and now ten years later there are four restaurants in Las Vegas.

The ribs are made the same way in Vegas as in Mills's other restaurants in Illinois, in a Southern Pride smoker over the mildly flavored apple wood that is plentiful in Murphysboro. But as in many cities new to 'cue, the food needed a little explaining. The menu now makes it clear that the pink layer on the meat is a "rosy cast"—not a sign that it's undercooked, but that it's been smoked on indirect heat in the pit.

Apple City Barbecue Sauce

The sauce is a family recipe, first created by Mike Mills's maternal grandmother. When he opened his debut restaurant, 17th Street, his mother, Faye, used to make this sauce by the gallon for the restaurant.

1 cup ketchup
2/3 cup seasoned rice vinegar
1/2 cup apple juice or cider
1/4 cup apple cider vinegar
1/2 cup packed brown sugar
1/4 cup soy sauce or Worcestershire sauce
2 teaspoons prepared yellow mustard
3/4 teaspoon garlic powder
1/4 teaspoon ground white pepper
1/4 teaspoon cayenne
1/3 cup bacon bits, ground in a spice grinder
1/3 cup peeled and grated apple
1/3 cup grated onion
2 teaspoons grated green bell pepper

Combine all ingredients, from the ketchup through the bacon bits, in a large saucepan, and then stir in the apple, onion, and bell pepper. Reduce heat and simmer uncovered for 10 to 15 minutes, or until the sauce thickens slightly, stirring frequently. Allow to cool, then pour it into sterilized glass bottles. The sauce will keep in refrigerator for up to 2 weeks and will flavor 2 racks of ribs.

GENERAL COOKIN' TIP

★ Place the ribs on your grill or smoker bone-side down. If at all possible, you want to leave them this way for their entire smoking time. You can achieve this by maintaining an even, constant temperature of between 225 and 250 degrees, whether you're using direct or indirect heat. If you must turn the ribs, do so as few times as possible to prevent the meat from drying out.

ROBB'S RIBBS

ALBUQUERQUE, NEW MEXICO

For Robb Richmond, pictured above, smoking meat started out as a hobby. He was trying to recapture the great barbecue he had as a kid, made by his favorite pit master, Old Man Cooper. After Cooper died, Richmond tried other barbecue, but he was always disappointed. Finally, Richmond decided to develop his own sauce and practiced with different wood in his backyard on a homemade smoker made out of an old hot water heater. This was the beginning of Richmond's experimentation with different woods —and his belief that certain woods go better with certain meats and sauces. For example, hickory wood better complements a sweet sauce, while pungent sauces work best with mesquite. Oak and apple wood is indigenous to the Southwest, hickory is plentiful in

Texas and Missouri. Richmond's ideal blend is a mixture of oak, hickory, pecan, and apple.

Richmond is a stickler for using the best ingredients. He uses natural pork with no antibiotics or growth hormones added, and prepares both St. Louis–cut and baby back ribs. His sauces, which pay tribute to the New Mexican predilection for hot pepper and come in both Original and Habanero, have twice won Best BBQ Sauce Award at the National Fiery Foods Show. Richmond started out gradually, with a four-table restaurant in 1988, and friends helping out with chores, like typing menus. Though it was a typo that turned ribs into "ribbs" in the name of the joint, the name stuck, resulting in Robb's motto: "If you're not eatin' ribbs with two Bs, you're just gettin' BS."

Robb's Ribbs BBQ Sauce

You can adjust the amount of chilies you use according to how much heat and spice you want in your dish.

$^1/_3$ cup peanut, vegetable, or safflower oil

1 teaspoon each chili caribe and fresh hot peppers (jalapeno or yellow hots)

1 small onion

5 cloves garlic, peeled

$^1/_3$ small lemon

$^1/_2$ cup brown sugar

2 tablespoons kosher or sea salt

1 tablespoon black pepper

1 tablespoon dry mustard

1 teaspoon cumin

1 teaspoon ground bay leaf

12 ounces beer

$^2/_3$ cup fresh lemon juice

1 cup each Worcestershire sauce, molasses, and cider vinegar

$1^1/_4$ cup each tomato paste, tomato sauce, and tomato ketchup

3 cups water

Coarsely chop the onion in a food processor. Finely chop the peeled garlic and lemon, including the rind. Mince the chilis, and sauté them in oil over moderate heat until they start to brown. Add the lemon, onion, and garlic to the chilis, and cook the mixture until the onion is transparent or light brown. (If you use caribe, the oil will get a red-brown color when the chilis are ready.) Add a mixture of the brown sugar, salt, pepper, dry mustard, cumin, and ground bay leaf, and cook about two minutes. Add the beer and cook for another few minutes. Add the non-tomato liquids and bring to a simmer, then add the tomato products. Bring it all to a simmer and cook for about one hour, or until all the flavors come together. This sauce will cover 8 racks of ribs.

WESTERN U.S. · KILLER RIBS

JOE'S REAL BBQ

GILBERT, ARIZONA

If any one thing captures the spirit of Joe's Real BBQ, it's Joe's annual Customer Appreciation Day, usually held the first Wednesday in May in honor of National Barbecue Month. One recent year, they served up free barbecue to over four-thousand people to thank them for their patronage. But this is just one way that Joe's pays tribute to their community.

In a previous life, Joe Johnston traveled extensively in Texas. He ended up with many favorite barbecue joints in the Lone Star State, and like those places that paid tribute to local history and culture, Joe wanted his own barbecue place to honor the small but fast-growing community of Gilbert, Arizona.

Joe enlisted former business partner Tim Peelen to join him in his new venture, and the two traveled the barbecue belt, visiting Houston, Dallas, and Memphis, to come up with their own style of barbecue. Recipes in hand, they turned their attention to their restaurant building, which was a church in its previous incarnation. They restored the original floors, kept the brick walls and awnings, and parked a 1948 John Deere tractor in the middle of the dining room as a reminder that Gilbert was once the hay capital of the world. There's also a mural entitled *The Fruit of Our Labor* hanging in the dining room that represents the agricultural history of the area.

Joe's Sweet Rub

1 cup granulated brown sugar

$1/2$ cup sugar

2 tablespoons granulated garlic

2 teaspoons black pepper

1 teaspoon cayenne pepper

1 teaspoon chili powder

2 teaspoons seasoned salt

$1/2$ teaspoon coriander

2 teaspoons dried oregano

Combine all the ingredients in a quart container with a tight-fitting lid. Roll to mix to avoid dust. Let this mixture settle for several minutes before generously sprinkling and rubbing it on both sides of the ribs. The rub can be applied immediately before cooking or up to several hours prior. It makes approximately 2 cups, enough to coat 8 to 10 slabs of ribs.

GENERAL COOKIN' TIPS

★ Joe and Tim use St. Louis–cut ribs, peeling away the membrane and applying a sweet rub, and smoke them at 195 degrees for $4^1/2$ hours. Pecan and mesquite are both native to Arizona, and Tim and Joe prefer the sweeter, milder flavor of pecan wood for smoking their pork ribs.

★ To select their smoker, they tasted meat cooked in every smoker available. They chose Oyler pits for a true Texas-style taste.

★ Joe's Real BBQ doesn't mop with any liquid at all during cooking, but they finish the ribs with sauce on top as they're served.

WESTERN U.S. ★ KILLER RIBS

MR. K'S BBQ

TUCSON, ARIZONA

You can find ribs in a lot of different environments— from a van parked on the side of the road or a wood-panel cabin with counter service to a backwoods shack or urban upscale restaurant, but you'll likely only ever encounter one barbecue joint that shares its space with a museum. Charles Kendrick, also known as Mr. K, first started selling Texas-style ribs in 1998 to support the Afro-American Heritage Museum, which he founded with Shad Blair. The two men, each avid collectors of African-American artifacts, decided to pool their collections. The barbecue was intended as a sideline to the museum, but the delectable smoked meat was soon in the limelight, the ribs quickly overtaking the museum as the main attraction.

A retired pharmacist, Kendrick received his first lessons in smoked meat as a teenager in East Texas more than sixty years ago when he helped his grandparents make real pit barbecue. In addition to his experience with his grandparents, Kendrick also took the "barbecue tour of Texas," occasionally, if he was lucky enough or persuasive enough, wrangling recipes from pit masters. "We're just as good as they are," Kendrick boasts, based on his experience in Texas.

The key to the flavor at Mr. K's, according to Kendrick, is that they cook the meat all the way with wood, using no gas at all. Hickory isn't native to Arizona, so they use mesquite at Mr. K's. For sauce, there's just one: a ketchup base with vinegar and honey. And for those Southwesterners addicted to heat? "If they want it hot, we hand them a bottle of hot sauce."

Mr. K's Rib Rub

Kendrick begins by massaging this rub into the meat well, and lets the ribs sit for at least 1 hour before cooking, though it's better if you can let them sit overnight. He never uses marinades or tenderizer. "We don't need it," he says. At Mr. K's, they smoke the ribs for 3 hours. You can tell it's done, Kendrick says, "if you grab one end and hold it up and it just starts separating from the bone."

1 cup salt
3 tablespoons coarsely ground black pepper
1 tablespoon dry oregano
1 tablespoon granulated garlic

Mix ingredients together and rub the mixture onto 4 slabs of ribs—it works just as well with beef and pork!

GENERAL COOKIN' TIPS

★ Try to follow the old-time traditional methods as much as possible. Cook only with wood (no gas starters), and use the best wood available. Don't cut the ribs before you smoke them because the meat will dry out.

★ Serve a sauce with a Texas-style ketchup base on the side. You can doctor the sauce however you like with vinegar, honey, and other spices.

KLONDIKE RIB & SALMON BBQ

──── WHITEHORSE, YUKON TERRITORY ────

Located near Alaska in the northwest Yukon Territory of Canada where the temperatures fall below zero in the fall and even lower in winter, it's not hard to imagine why Klondike Rib and Salmon BBQ is only a seasonal business, operating from May to September. This may sound like a great schedule, but Trevor Amiot and Dona Novecosky, the hardworking husband-and-wife team behind the joint, don't take the rest of the year off; they also own and operate Beez Kneez Bakpakers, a year-round hostel for world travelers.

Amiot and Novecosky, pictured above, bought the restaurant's building five years ago, but they can't alter the structure—a walled tent with a tin frame and two patios—too much because it's a historic landmark, as well as the oldest operating building in Whitehorse. Amiot learned how to smoke wild game, fish, and "all kinds of stuff" from his parents, who enjoyed cooking big family dinners while he was growing up in British Columbia. He does the same kind of home-style cooking at his popular restaurant. He rubs pork ribs with crushed peppercorns, smokes them over hickory and cherry wood for six to eight hours, then slow cooks them in the oven for two hours. The final step is to finish them on the grill with a tomato-based molasses-and-vinegar-flavored barbecue sauce. But "it's the smoke that gives it all its flavor," Amiot said, so much so that he also smokes sockeye salmon, halibut, steaks, and vegetables.

Klondike Yukon Ribs

1 rack pork spareribs
Salt
Ground peppercorns
Your favorite tomato-based barbecue sauce

Rub ribs gently all over with the salt and ground peppercorns, then smoke the ribs over cherry and hickory smoke for approximately 6 hours. Remove the rack from the smoker and transfer them to your oven. Bake at 400 degrees for 2 hours, or until the meat is falling off the bone.

Remove the ribs from the oven and let cool. Once they are cool, scrape the fat and back skin off the ribs. Then smother the ribs in barbecue sauce and grill for 20 minutes until sauce is caramelized.

GENERAL COOKIN' TIPS

★ Remove the fat and back skin from the ribs by parboiling, especially if you aren't going to smoke them. Do so before putting the ribs on the grill (after cooking them in the oven), otherwise you'll burn the ribs.

★ The bold flavor of hickory wood is mellowed by mixing it with sweet cherry wood.

★ Smoke gives the desired flavor, while additional time in the oven helps the meat fall off the bone, and grilling at the end finishes it off with a nice layer of caramelized sauce.

PALOMINO SMOKEHOUSE AND SOCIAL CLUB

CALGARY, ALBERTA

Before Fred Konopaki opened the Palomino Smokehouse in 2005, he was a partner in another dining establishment, The Belvedere, in Calgary. Eager for a change, he considered his options and developed his next concept. Given Alberta's famous beef and cowboy culture, it seemed logical to open a barbecue restaurant. So he visited Memphis Blues in Vancouver and spent some time in Nashville and Memphis. There, he trained in the art of barbecue with Lee McWright, a championship barbecuer with a degree in food science and "more trophies than I've ever seen," according to Konopaki.

Konopaki is proud of his Ole Hickory smoker, which he had shipped in from Missouri. It weighed so much it had to be installed with a crane, and it can cook up to 750 pounds of meat at one time. Palomino chef Jody Barned, nicknamed the "Barbecue Queen," smokes the meat over predominately Okanagan, British Columbia, apple wood, for sweet smoke and a bona fide smoke ring.

The free-standing brick building that houses the Palomino is a rarity in Calgary. Konopaki left the former furniture store's original floor and decorated the joint with posters he picked up in Nashville, including his favorite, a giant picture of Johnny Cash flipping the bird. As for barbecue wisdom, Konopaki believes that there's a tendency to mystify barbecue, but he wants to keep it simple. "If you add one more ingredient, it'll still taste good," he said. But he does believe that Canada has at least one advantage over the United States—"Our beef is better," he says.

Smoked Alberta Prime Rib Bones

Saskatoon Berry Barbecue Sauce

2 cups fresh Saskatoon berries (or wild blueberries, in a pinch)

1 cup sugar

$\frac{1}{4}$ cup beef stock

1 medium onion, minced

1 teaspoon fresh ginger, minced

2 tablespoons butter

1 teaspoon allspice

$\frac{1}{2}$ cup balsamic vinegar

2 tablespoons tamarind paste

Salt and pepper to taste

Rocky Mountain Rib Rub

$\frac{1}{4}$ cup allspice

$\frac{1}{4}$ cup packed brown sugar

$\frac{1}{4}$ cup granulated garlic

$\frac{1}{4}$ cup kosher salt

2 tablespoons nutmeg

2 tablespoons cinnamon

1 teaspoon ground juniper berry

Rocky Mountain Rib Mop

1 cup maple syrup

4 cups dark beer (not stout)

Place the berries, sugar, and beef stock in a saucepan and bring to a boil, then simmer. Sweat onions and ginger in butter, and add allspice. Add balsamic vinegar, then the onions and ginger, plus tamarind paste, to the berry mixture. Season with salt and pepper and set aside. Combine all the ingredients for the rib rub. Rub the back and front of two whole prime rib racks with the rib rub and shake off the excess. Combine all the ingredients for the rib mop. Cook the ribs at 220 degrees for about 8 hours, basting with the mop while the ribs are smoking. After the ribs are cooked, slather on the berry sauce or serve it on the side.

BIG T'S BBQ & SMOKEHOUSE

CALGARY, ALBERTA

Karen Ingram, a restaurateur with thirty years experience, had a hunch that people in Calgary would like to eat barbecue. She knew about the Canadian Barbecue Association and that there were plenty of barbecue competitions in Canada, but she didn't really know of too many restaurants Calgary diners could go to for wood-smoked meats. Ingram's own experience with barbecue came from traveling around the United States with her parents when she was a child. Of everything on that trip, the barbecue left the strongest impression, and she never forgot the taste, especially of Texan 'cue. Before opening their first barbecue joint, Karen's daughter, Nicky, traveled around the Southern United States for eighteen months, tasting barbecue everywhere from Memphis to Texas. When they first started out, they had to experiment and found there was a lot of trial and error—locals thought the meat was too smoky, so they cut back on the amount of smoke.

Big T's serves up all kinds of ribs: St. Louis cut, baby backs, rib ends, and even gigantic beef bones. Everything is made from scratch, including the side dishes, barbecue sauces, and several different rubs. They let the rub sit on the ribs overnight, then smoke them over hickory and apple wood from British Columbia's Okanagan Valley. It's a good thing that Ingram followed her intuition: Her 'cue caught on so quickly that she was able to open three locations in one year, and all have the same casual, fun atmosphere with plastic red-checkered tablecloths and paper menus, draft beers, bourbon, and lots of big parties.

Big T's Maple Bourbon Barbecue Sauce

¼ cup butter

1 tablespoon canola oil

2½ cups medium onions, finely diced

1¼ cups apple cider vinegar

¾ cup molasses

1¼ cups Canadian maple syrup

½ cup Jim Beam White Label bourbon

1½ cups ketchup

1¼ cups orange juice

¼ cup Worcestershire

1¼ teaspoons black pepper

3 teaspoons salt

Melt the butter in a large saucepan, and add in the oil. Sauté the onions until they're translucent. Add the vinegar, molasses, and maple syrup and stir until dissolved, then add the rest of the ingredients. Stir over medium heat until all the ingredients are well blended, and bring to a boil. Then, lower the heat and simmer for 30 minutes. Slather sauce on 2 slabs of ribs or serve it warm on the side.

GENERAL COOKIN' TIPS

★ Buy good-quality ribs and keep in mind that every rack of ribs is different and cooks in a slightly different way, so take the time to look after each rack individually.

★ You can learn to tell when ribs are done by looking and touching. Grab the rack with tongs and twist it a bit. If the ribs are done, the meat will break away from the bone.

★ Use real maple syrup in the sauce—imitations just don't work.

MUDDY WATERS SMOKEHOUSE

WINNIPEG, MANITOBA

What could be more appropriate than a smokehouse with the same name as blues legend Muddy Waters? Though the association is a fortuitous one, the muddy waters of this name can be traced to the restaurant's location at the Forks, where two rivers converge and mud is churned up. In addition, the name Winnipeg actually means "muddy waters" in the aboriginal tongue, adding authenticity to the fitting name of this joint. And of course, they play blues music to match the Memphis-style barbecue served here.

Doug Stephen, president of a Winnipeg restaurant group, was inspired by his travels in Alabama, Tennessee, and Kentucky to open Muddy Waters. In 1998, when they first opened, Southern-style barbecue was a rare commodity in Manitoba. "There are lots of people who do ribs in their backyard on the grill, but we want to get Canadians used to 'low and slow,'" he said, referring to cooking over indirect heat and infusing the meat with wood smoke.

On the outside, the smokehouse is composed of sleek, modern glass, but on the inside there's a Southern flair and a down-home feeling, complete with raw wood beams, old license plates, and walls on which visitors can sign their names. Though the airy and spacious space holds only 65 seats inside, the place comes alive in the summer with 140 seats outside on patios overlooking the river.

Muddy Waters BBQ Sauce

¹/₃ cup packed brown sugar

2 teaspoons chili powder

1 teaspoon dry mustard

¹/₂ teaspoon ground ginger

¹/₅ teaspoon cayenne

³/₄ teaspoon black pepper

3 ¹/₂ ounces white vinegar

1 ³/₄ tablespoons molasses

1 ³/₄ tablespoons water

1 ¹/₃ cups ketchup

In a large stainless steel pot combine the first six ingredients. Add vinegar, molasses, and water, and stir until they're dissolved, then add the ketchup and mix. Bring to a boil over high heat, stirring constantly. Reduce heat and simmer for 30 minutes, and then remove the pot from the heat and let the sauce cool to room temperature. Covers 1 rack of ribs.

GENERAL COOKIN' TIPS

★ Cook ribs for 2¹/₂ hours at 180 to 200 degrees. Once the meat is removed from the smoker at Muddy Waters, the ribs are sauced and flash-cooked on the grill.

★ Canadian beef has a different flavor than American USDA. In Canada, the cows are fed barley instead of corn, and it's a difference you can taste.

★ The ribs at Muddy Waters Smokehouse are served with their moderately spiced barbecue sauce or a mango-chili sauce, which is enhanced with mango puree and hot chilis.

★ All the meat is smoked over hickory and oak in a Cookshack smoker that hails from Oklahoma. Oak burns at a high temperature, and when you get it down to coal, its embers last longer.

DUSTY'S BAR & BBQ

— WHISTLER, BRITISH COLUMBIA —

Located at the foot of Whistler Mountain, Dusty's Bar has a decades-long history as a place for fun après-ski partying. In 2000, the old place, a collection of trailers with a leaking roof, was replaced by a new building with restaurant facilities. The staff thought that barbecue would be a fantastic addition to the Whistler area, so they went on a three-week barbecue road trip in the United States, traveling from Kansas to the Southwest and eating three meals of smoked meat a day. And though the current two-story building is new, the structure was built with wood from an old bridge and has rustic appeal to spare. A look around the inside reveals exposed posts and beams, a hardwood dance floor, and fireplaces both indoors and outside on the patio. The patio, which wraps around the building, is the perfect place to watch the pit masters at work.

Though they serve their mouth-watering smoked ribs all week, chef Rob Shortreed and his staff fire up the outdoor smoker, a closed pit manufactured in Texas, on Saturdays and make what they call "competition ribs." It's a chance to "work on our game," says Shortreed, in preparation for competitions in the Pacific Northwest, Calgary, and other locations. When they're smoking outdoors, Shortreed and his crew experiment with different flavors, but during the week, they use their favorite rub, a well-balanced mixture with a Southwestern flavor.

Dusty's BBQ Rub

Shortreed's rule of thumb when making a rub is to use set proportions—one third each of salt, sugar, and seasoning. He recommends that you use your favorite spices to make the seasoning, or use the recipe below.

$\frac{1}{2}$ cup seasoning (a combination of the following)

> **Celery seed**
>
> **Garlic**
>
> **Onion powder**
>
> **Allspice**
>
> **Cumin**
>
> **Cayenne**
>
> **Black pepper**
>
> **Paprika**
>
> **Turmeric**

$\frac{1}{2}$ cup sugar, half white and half brown

$\frac{1}{2}$ cup salt

Make your seasoning by combining the spices to taste and blending well, then mix it with the sugar and salt. This rub will flavor 6 racks of ribs.

GENERAL COOKIN' TIPS

★ For a special barbecue sauce, you can buy a store-bought brand and enhance it with your favorite alcohol (Jack Daniel's works well) and maple syrup.

★ To create your own smoker, use a pan with wood chips. Soak the chips in water until they're damp, place them in a disposable aluminum cooking pan, cover with foil, and put the pan on a stove burner until the chips are smoldering. Once they're ready, poke a few holes in the aluminum foil covering and place the pan in the bottom of your oven. Put the meat on a baking sheet on an upper rack in the oven, and cook it for about $2\frac{1}{2}$ hours at 250 to 275 degrees.

KANSAS CITY BAR.B.Q. SHACK
BURNABY, BRITISH COLUMBIA

Located in a modern forty-eight-lane bowling center, Kansas City Bar.B.Q., which pays tribute to Kansas City as the "smokehouse capital," was conceived as a perfect match for bowling. Instead of being limited to a snack bar with French fries and grilled cheese, bowlers at Revs, Burnaby's popular bowling center, can take a break and sit down for a meal of smoked meat instead. You don't have to bowl to eat, though. Anyone can order the generous portions of ribs and their hot side dishes and listen to the food-appropriate blues music. The setting is a contemporary smokehouse with hardwood floors, shiny red lacquer tables, and chalk portraits of B.B. King, Jimi Hendrix, and Robert Plant adorning the large windows.

Kansas City Bar.B.Q. offer sauces with regional flavors from all over the United States, including a hot and spicy Midwest/Kansas City sauce; a Pacific Northwest honey-barbecue sauce, a smoky Southwest sauce with a little Texan flair added, and a Southeast City Sauce, a mustard-based sauce similar to what you'll find in South Carolina. They smoke their ribs over alder wood, which is prevalent in Northwest Canada. In addition, the folks here are determined to educate Canadians about real smokehouse barbecue and to distinguish what they do from backyard grilling. To their customers, they explain their slow-cooking methods using smoke, the "pink" hue on the outside of the meat, the smoke ring that shows the effects of wood smoke, and the "bark" that develops on the outside of the meat when it's penetrated by smoke—all signs that this is the real deal.

Kansas City Bar.B.Q. Shack Smokehouse Ribs

3 to 4 racks pork ribs
Dry rub
    $\frac{1}{4}$ cup packed brown sugar
    2 tablespoons paprika
    2 tablespoons cayenne pepper
    $1\frac{1}{2}$ tablespoons salt
    2 tablespoons chili powder
    2 tablespoons garlic powder
    2 tablespoons onion powder
$1\frac{1}{2}$ cups barbecue sauce

Place pork ribs in a deep metal pan and pour enough boiling water into the pan to cover the ribs. Cover the pan with aluminum foil and place it in the oven at 400 degrees for 2 hours, then remove the pan and set it aside. Combine the dry rub ingredients and mix to taste. Gently apply the rub onto the ribs and wrap them tightly in aluminum foil. (You can keep them in the refrigerator until needed.)

Set your smoker to 225 degrees and place the ribs onto a rack, smoking the ribs for 1 hour. After the hour is up, brush barbecue sauce onto the ribs and smoke them for another 20 minutes. Remove the ribs from the smoke and enjoy!

GENERAL COOKIN' TIPS

★ To achieve the falling-off-the-bone quality preferred by many Canadians, Kansas City Bar.B.Q. Shack boils pork ribs with garlic for 2 hours before putting them in the smoker.

★ For best results, avoids dramatic spikes in temperature when smoking the meat, and keep the cooking temperature between 185 and 225 degrees.

MEMPHIS BLUES BARBECUE HOUSE

VANCOUVER, BRITISH COLUMBIA

Park Heffelfinger and George Siu, pictured above, were professional foodies—self-proclaimed "food geeks"—who met in a wine class, but it wasn't until they took a trip to Memphis together that they discovered their love for barbecue. Heffelfinger's background was in wine, and he was the director and founder of the Vancouver Wine Academy, while George Siu had a background in restaurant management, including owning and operating a restaurant.

At first, their barbecue epiphany took the form of backyard barbecue parties for friends. And although one of their friends advised them to open their own restaurant, it wasn't until they attended the Memphis in May World Championship and met an experienced team

from Little Rock, Arkansas, that Siu and Heffelfinger's barbecue dreams became more than half-baked. With the help of this team, the two learned some tricks of the trade and came home with a multitude of menu ideas. Four months later, they opened, serving a hybrid of what they had tasted in Memphis, based on what they liked best. Their goal was Memphis-style barbecue, dry smoked with dry rub and sauce on the side. They smoke their meat in an Ole Hickory pit, mostly over aromatic woods—sometimes maple or black walnut, but usually apple. Though there wasn't too much local awareness of barbecue when they opened, soon after they found that people flocked to Memphis Blues to enjoy big piles of meat in a relaxed setting.

Memphis Blues BBQ Ribs

Memphis Blues's own patented sauce is straight out of Memphis. Their customers consume it by the gallon, but this recipe makes approximately 3 cups.

Memphis Blues BBQ Sauce
- 1 10-ounce can tomato paste
- 1/2 cup packed brown sugar
- 1/2 cup molasses
- 1/4 cup honey
- 1/4 cup soy sauce
- 1/2 cup French's mustard
- 3 tablespoons garlic powder
- 3 tablespoons onion powder
- 1/4 cup Worcestershire sauce
- 1/4 cup white vinegar
- 1 cup ketchup
- 3 tablespoons Durkey's Hot Sauce
- 1 teaspoon salt
- 2 cups water

1 slab pork side ribs
1/2 cup dry rub of your choice

Add the sauce ingredients to a pot and cook over low heat, whisking thoroughly until smooth. Simmer for 30 minutes, but be careful not to burn it. Store in your refrigerator for up to one week.

Rub the meat thoroughly with a basic dry rub, and place it in the refrigerator for 1 hour. Put the ribs in a homemade smoker box at medium-high heat, and cook for approximately 4 to 4 1/2 hours, turning the ribs a few times for even cooking. Pull two of the ribs apart to see if they tear apart easily and to check the color of the meat—it should have a pink color from the smoke. Apply the barbecue sauce, or serve it on the side—whichever you prefer.

DIX BARBECUE AND BREWERY

VANCOUVER, BRITISH COLUMBIA

Located directly across from the football stadium and close to the hockey stadium in Vancouver, Dix Barbecue and Brewery is the ideal place for hungry fans to chow down on hearty ribs before and after the games, or during, as they watch the big-screen televisions. In between the activity, though, the TVs are turned off, and candlelight and blues music set a down-South mood, complete with dark wood and checkered tablecloths. The ribs are cooked Southern style, to complement this ambiance and as a homage to pit master Richard Harding's favorite approach to barbecue.

Beef and St. Louis pork ribs are slow-cooked on a Southern Pride smoker over apple and hickory woods at 180 to 200 degrees for the distinctive pink color that can be produced only by real wood smoke. Harding, who picked up his barbecue skills in the kitchen at Dix, promises that, "Ribs aren't the same if they're not smoked. Boiling takes the flavor out of it. Then you just taste the barbecue sauce." Many Canadians are used to boiled ribs with meat falling off the bone, but it's looking up for true barbecue, if the game crowds are any indication. Harding's beef ribs with a rich, dark Texas Whiskey sauce, made with coffee and molasses, and pork ribs with a sweet and tangy Carolina tomato-based red sauce, prepared with coffee and vinegar, are catching on fast.

Dix Barbecue Smoked Beef Ribs

Mustard mop

- 3 cups dark beer
- 7 cups yellow mustard
- 1 cup Dijon mustard
- 2 tablespoons hot sauce
- $1/4$ cup packed brown sugar
- 1 tablespoon salt
- 1 tablespoon pepper

Rib rub

- $1\,1/4$ cups smoked paprika
- 1 cup packed brown sugar
- $1/2$ cup salt
- $1/2$ cup garlic powder
- $1/4$ cup onion powder
- $1/4$ cup celery salt
- 3 tablespoons ground black pepper
- 3 tablespoons ground coriander
- 3 tablespoons mustard powder
- 2 tablespoons ground cumin
- 1 tablespoon cayenne pepper

12 racks of ribs

Combine all the ingredients for the mustard mop in a bowl; set aside. Combine all the ingredients for the rib rub in a separate bowl; set aside. Generously slather the mustard mop all over the de-membraned ribs, and then sprinkle the rub on the ribs until they're fully covered. Smoke the ribs using young apple wood chips in a carefully monitored 200-degree smoker for at least 6 to 8 hours, or until a thermometer inserted into the meat reads 180 degrees. Remove the ribs from the smoker and let them stand at room temperature for 10 minutes, then serve.

CANADA
KILLER RIBS

MIKE LOVE'S BARBEQUE & SMOKEHOUSE

BARRIE, ONTARIO

In his previous career, Mike Perley's job frequently took him to the United States's barbecue belt—namely Kansas City, Atlanta, and Texas—where on one two-day trip, he managed to eat barbecue four times at four different restaurants. His newfound passion culminated when he flew back from the South to Toronto and went right to his local hardware store to buy his first smoker. Then, in 2003, he decided he needed a career change. "I wanted to pioneer this type of food in this part of the province," he said. "Our ribfest up here—the Barrie Ribfest—shows that it's definitely catching on." While others nearby are making oven-baked ribs, Perley is interested in traditional wood-smoked barbecue.

Perley is a fan of Kansas City 'cue—he thinks it's "the best on the planet"—so he created a Kansas City–style sauce with tomatoes, vinegar, molasses, hot pepper sauce, mustard, water, allspice, chili powder, cinnamon, curry, mace, paprika, black pepper, garlic powder, salt, white sugar, brown sugar, and cayenne pepper. It's the allspice, cinnamon, and mace that gives the sauce a distinctive KC taste. The wood Perley uses to smoke his meat on depends on what he's cooking, but he favors cherry, apple, or red oak. He believes the food tastes better when it's made by the owner of a restaurant. "You can taste the chef's passion," he said. And in case you can't tell, the name of his restaurant makes it clear that Mike Loves Barbeque.

Mike Love's Barbeque Rib Dry Rub

This is the rub recipe that helped Perley take first place in the ribs division at the 2005 Barrie Ribfest.

$1/4$ cup black pepper

$1/4$ cup paprika

3 tablespoons turbinado sugar (raw sugar)

1 tablespoon kosher salt

1 tablespoon chili powder

2 tablespoons granulated garlic

2 tablespoons onion powder

$1/4$ teaspoon lemon pepper

Combine all the ingredients and mix well. Apply the dry rub to 2 racks of ribs 1 hour before smoking, and smoke at 225 degrees until tender. (It usually takes Mike Love's 4 hours.) You can tell the ribs are done when the meat pulls back from the bone by at least $1/4$ inch. Another test is to pick up the rack in the middle—if the meat starts to crack open, pull them off the smoker, and hit the dinner bell.

GENERAL COOKIN' TIPS

★ Buy the right equipment for backyard smoking. "Don't waste money on something cheap you are just going to pitch because it doesn't work," advises Perley.

★ Don't use too much wood right off the bat. It's a challenge to get the fire to a constant temperature, so experiment with how much charcoal or wood you need and see how long it will burn. "Cherry is my favorite," Perley says. "It gives ribs a beautiful, burnt red look, and a subtle, sweet flavor. You can taste the difference."

★ It doesn't make any difference in the taste if you marinate or rub your ribs 24 hours versus 1 hour before you put them in the pit because the smoke negates the overnight marinating. On the other hand, if you are grilling or oven roasting, marinating overnight adds great flavor.

PHIL'S ORIGINAL BBQ

TORONTO, ONTARIO

In 1990, when Phil Nyman heard that his friend was traveling all the way from Toronto to Memphis, Tennessee, just to eat barbecue, he really didn't understand why anyone would trek so far just to eat. But his friend's experience peaked his interest, and a few months later, Nyman made his own pilgrimage to the barbecue belt, visiting Kentucky, Tennessee, Missouri, and Illinois. When he returned home, he started experimenting with smokers in his backyard, beginning with a Weber water smoker and moving up to an Oklahoma Joe barrel smoker. He had experience as a cook in restaurants around Toronto, and although there was a vast range of ethnic foods, there was no one doing real barbecue in his community. For the first six years, he catered, doing all the cooking in his backyard, but in 1998, he opened his own restaurant.

Phil's Original Barbecue is a fifty-seat joint with Formica tabletops, exposed brick walls, and photographs of blues players and jazzmen on the walls, and Nyman plays music to match. "I try to support local artists, even though there's not enough room for live music," he says. If you ask Nyman which regional barbecue style he follows, the answer depends on where you come from. One time while he was telling a woman from Kansas City that his ribs were Memphis style, a woman from Memphis overheard him and he had to do some "fast stepping." His favorite customer comment: "Your barbecue is as good as what we get at home."

Hosers' Ribs

Nyman's pork ribs pay tribute to the country boys of the Great White North; they're beer-soaked and Canadian.

2 tablespoons chopped garlic
1 cup packed brown sugar
1 12-ounce bottle or can dark beer
2 slabs of side ribs, St. Louis–cut
Rub mix of your choice

Combine the garlic, sugar, and beer in a large freezer bag, and mix well. Strip the membrane off the back of the ribs. Put the ribs in the bag of marinade, and squeeze all the air out. Seal and refrigerate overnight.

One hour before cooking time, take the bag out of the refrigerator, pat the ribs dry, and sprinkle with your favorite rub. Let them sit at room temperature. Cook over indirect heat over fruitwood fire (apple, peach, cherry, or pear) at 225 degrees for about $3\frac{1}{2}$ to 4 hours. You can tell the ribs are done when the meat pulls away from the end of bones. Cut ribs into individual ribs, and lightly shake on some more rub before serving.

GENERAL COOKIN' TIPS

★ Be patient and take notes. When Nyman was first starting out and experimenting, he made delicious barbecue, but didn't know what he had done or how to repeat it to achieve the same results. Pay attention to what ingredients you put in your rub, how much heat you use, techniques for keeping the temperature steady, and where you put the meat on the smoker to get the best results.

★ Practice, practice, practice!

INDEX

Restaurant names are in *italic*.

A

Alberta Smoked Prime Rib Bones, 93
Allen & Son (Chapel Hill, North Carolina), 56-57
Allen & Son Sweet and Tangy Sauce, 57
Alligator (Gator) Ribs, "Eat or Be Eaten" Bodacious BBQ, 69
Almost "The Original Q Shack" Rib Rub, 55
Apple City Barbecue Sauce, 83
Arousing Rib Rub, Roscoe's, 31
Arthur Bryant's Barbecue (Kansas City, Missouri), 42, 46-47
Arthur Bryant's Rib Rub, 47

B

Baby back ribs
    Buffalo Bob's Fantastic BBQ Back Ribs, 49
    Slow-Roasted Ribs, 35
Barbecue Joint, The (Chapel Hill, North Carolina), 58-59
Barbecue Joint Spareribs, The, 59
BBQ Back Ribs, Buffalo Bob's Fantastic, 49
Beef ribs
    American USDA vs. Canadian beef, 97
    Beef Short Ribs, 15
    Blue Smoke Black Pepper Beef Ribs, 21
    Dix Barbecue's Smoked Beef Ribs, 105
    Salt Lick-Style Beef Ribs, 65
    Smoked Alberta Prime Rib Bones, 93
Big Bob Gibson Bar-B-Que (Decatur, Alabama), 62-63
Big Ed's Marinade, 25
Big T's BBQ & Smokehouse (Calgary, Alberta), 94-95
Big T's Maple Bourbon Barbecue Sauce, 95
Black Pepper Beef Ribs, Blue Smoke, 21
Blue Smoke (New York, New York), 20-21
Blue Smoke Black Pepper Beef Ribs, 21
Bodacious "Eat or Be Eaten" BBQ Gator Ribs, 69
Bourbon Maple Barbecue Sauce, Big T's, 95
Bubbalou's Bodacious Bar-B-Que (Winter Park, Florida), 68-69
Buffalo Bob's Fantastic BBQ Back Ribs, 49
Buffalo Bob's Smokehouse (Lawrence, Kansas), 48-49

C

Canada killer ribs, 90-109
Cherry Coke BBQ Sauce, 27
Chubby's Barbeque (Emmitsburg, Maryland), 28-29
Cozy Corner Restaurant (Memphis, Tennessee), 60-61

D

Desiree Robinson's Home-Cooked Pork Ribs, 61
Dinosaur Bar-B-Que (Syracuse, New York), 12-13
Dix Barbecue and Brewery (Vancouver, British Columbia), 104-105
Dix Barbecue Smoked Beef Ribs, 105
Dixie Bones (Woodbridge, Virginia), 50-51
Dry rubs, *see also* Rubs
    Almost "The Original Q Shack" Rib Rub, 55
    Barbecue Joint's Spare Ribs, The, 59
    Kansas City Bar.B.Q. Shack's Smokehouse Ribs, 101
    Mike Loves Barbecue's Rib Dry Rub, 107
    Mrs. Head's Spare Ribs, 51
    Paul Kirk's Dry Rub, 23
    Uncle Willie's Dry Rub, 19
Dusty's BBQ (Whistler, British Columbia), 98-99
Dusty's BBQ Rub, 99

E

Eagle Rib Shack (Boise, Idaho), 76-77
"Eat or Be Eaten" Bodacious Bar-B-Que Gator Ribs, 69

F

Finkerman's Bar-B-Q Sauce, 11
Finkerman's Riverside Bar-B-Q (Montpelier, Vermont), 10-11

G

Garlic-Honey Tomato Glaze, 63
Gates Rib Seasoning, 45
Gates Bar-B-Q (Kansas City, Missouri), 44-45
Gator Ribs, "Eat or Be Eaten" Bodacious BBQ, 69
Glaze, Honey-Garlic Tomato, 63

H

Hawaiian Ribs, 29
Herb Rub, Smoked Lamb Spareribs with, 77
Hickory Park (Ames, Iowa), 38-39
Hickory Park Ribs, 39
Holy Smokes BBQ & Whole Hog House (West Hatfield, Massachusetts), 14-15
Home-Cooked Pork Ribs, Desiree Robinson's, 61
Honey
    Honey-Garlic Tomato Glaze, 63
    Honey-Mustard Ribs, 73
    Jones Honey-Barbecue Sauce, 71
Hosers' Ribs, 109

J

Joe's Real BBQ (Gilbert, Arizona), 86-87
Joe's Sweet Rub, 87
Jones Barbecue (Seattle, Washington), 70-71
Jones Honey-Barbecue Sauce, 71

K

Kansas City Bar.B.Q. Shack (Burnaby, British Columbia), 100-101
Kansas City Bar.B.Q. Shack Smokehouse Ribs, 101
Klondike Rib & Salmon BBQ (Whitehorse, Yukon), 90-91
Klondike Yukon Ribs, 91

L

Lamb ribs
    Lamb Spareribs with Herb Rub, 77
    Moonlite Bar-B-Q Mutton Ribs, 53
    Smoked Lamb Spareribs with Herb Rub, 77
Lemon Ribs, 79
LJ's BBQ (Pawtucket, Rhode Island), 16-17
LJ's Pork Rib Rub, 17

M

Maple Bourbon Barbecue Sauce, Big T's, 95
Marinades
    Big Ed's Marinade, 25
    Mrs. Head's Spare Ribs, 51
    Pineapple Marinated Loin Back Pork Ribs, 63
Market Ribs, Smitty's, 67
Memphis Blues Barbecue House (Vancouver, British Columbia), 102-103
Memphis Blues BBQ Ribs, 103
Memphis Championship Barbecue (Las Vegas, Nevada), 82-83
Memphis Minnie's Rib Rub, 81
Memphis Minnie's (San Francisco, California), 80-81
Midwestern U.S. killer ribs, 30-49
Mike Love's Barbecue & Smokehouse (Barrie, Ontario), 106-107
Mike Love's Barbecue Rib Dry Rub, 107

Mojo Rib Rub, Smoke Daddy's, 37
Moonlite Bar-B-Q Inn (Owensboro, Kentucky), 52-53
Moonlite Bar-B-Q Mutton Ribs, 53
Mops
    Mustard Mop, 105
    Rocky Mountain Rib Mop, 93
Mr. K's BBQ (Tucson, Arizona), 88-89
Mr. K's Rib Rub, 89
Mrs. Head's Spareribs, 51
Muddy Waters BBQ Sauce, 97
Muddy Waters Smokehouse (Winnipeg, Manitoba), 96-97
Mustard
    Honey-Mustard Ribs, 73
    Mustard Mop, 105
    Oklahoma Joe's Mustard Rib Rub, 43
Mutha Sauce, 13
Mutton Ribs, Moonlite Bar-B-Q, 53

N
Northeastern U.S. killer ribs, 10-29

O
Oklahoma Joe's Barbecue (Kansas City, Kansas), 42-43
Oklahoma Joe's Tasty Ribs, 43
Original Big Ed's BBQ, The (Old Bridge, New Jersey), 24-25
Original Q Shack, The (Durham, North Carolina), 54-55

P
Palomino Smokehouse and Social Club (Calgary, Alberta), 92-93
Paul Kirk's Dry Rub, 23
Phil's Original BBQ (Toronto, Ontario), 108-109
Pineapple-Marinated Loin Back Pork Ribs with Honey-Garlic Tomato Glaze, 63
Pork ribs
    Desiree Robinson's Home-Cooked Pork Ribs, 61
    Hawaiian Ribs, 29
    Hosers' Ribs, 109
    Kansas City Bar.B.Q. Shack's Smokehouse Ribs, 101
    Klondike's Yukon Ribs, 91
    LJ's Pork Rib Rub, 17
    Memphis Blues' BBQ Ribs, 103
    Memphis Minnie's Rib Rub, 81
    Pineapple Marinated Loin Back Pork Ribs with Honey-Garlic Tomato Glaze, 63
    Roscoe's Favorite Ribs, 31
Prestigious Barbecue Society Rib Rub, The, 41
Prime Rib Bones, Smoked Alberta, 93

Q
Q4U (West Valley, Utah), 78-79

R
Road House BBQ (Eagle, Idaho), 74-75
Road House Rub, 75
Robb's Ribb BBQ Sauce, 85
Robb's Ribs (Albuquerque, New Mexico), 84-85
Rocky Mountain Rib Rub, 93
Roscoe's Arousing Rib Rub, 31
Roscoe's Favorite Ribs, 31
Roscoe's Root Beer & Ribs (Rochester, Minnesota), 30-31
R.U.B. (Righteous Urban Barbecue) (New York, New York), 22-23
Rubs, *see also* Dry rubs
    Arthur Bryant's Rib Rub, 47
    Blue Smoke Black Pepper Beef Ribs, 21
    Dix Barbecue's Smoked Beef Ribs, 105
    Dusty's Barbecue Rub, 99
    Herb Rub, 77
    Joe's Sweet Rub, 87
    LJ's Pork Rib Rub, 17

Memphis Minnie'e Rib Rub, 81
Mr. K's Rib Rub, 89
Oklahoma Joe's Mustard Rib Rub, 43
Prestigious Barbecue Society Rib Rub, The, 41
Road House Rub, 75
Robb's Ribb Rubb, 85
Rocky Mountain Rib Rub, 93
Roscoe's Arousing Rib Rub, 31
Smoke Daddy's Mojo Rib Rub, 37

S
Salt Lick, The (Driftwood, Texas), 64-65
Salt Lick-Style Beef Ribs, 65
Saskatoon Berry Barbecue Sauce, 93
Sauces
    Allen & Sons Sweet and Tangy Sauce, 57
    Apple City Barbecue Sauce, 83
    Barbecue Joint's Spare Ribs, The, 59
    Big T's Maple Bourbon Barbecue Sauce, 95
    Cherry Coke BBQ Sauce, 27
    Finkerman's BBQ Sauce, 11
    Honey-Mustard Ribs, 73
    Jones Honey-Barbecue Sauce, 71
    Lemon Sauce, 79
    Memphis Blues Barbecue Sauce, 103
    Muddy Waters BBQ Sauce, 97
    Mutha Sauce, 13
    Saskatoon Berry Barbecue Sauce, 93
Seasoning, Gates' Rib, 45
Short Ribs, Beef, 15
Simple and Delicious BBQ Rib Recipe, Smoky Jon's, 33
Slow-Roasted Ribs, 35
Smitty's Market (Lockhart, Texas), 66-67
Smitty's Market Ribs, 67
Smoke Daddy, The (Chicago, Illinois), 36-37
Smoke Daddy Mojo Rib Rub, The 37
Smoked Alberta Prime Rib Bones, 93
Smoked Lamb Spareribs with Herb Rub, 77
Smoky Jon's #1 BBQ (Madison, Wisconsin), 32-33
Smoky Jon's Simple and Delicious BBQ Rib Recipe, 33
Southern U.S. killer ribs, 50-69
Spare ribs
    Barbecue Joint's Spare Ribs, The, 59
    Mrs. Head's Spare Ribs, 51
    Smitty's Market Ribs, 67
    Smoked Lamb Spareribs with Herb Rub, 77
St. Louis-style ribs, 17, 27, 55
Sweet and Tangy Sauce, Allen & Sons, 57

T
Tangy and Sweet Sauce, Allen & Sons, 57
Tomato Honey-Garlic Glaze, 63
Tommy Gunn's American Barbeque (Philadelphia, Pennsylvania), 26-27
Twin Anchors Restaurant & Tavern (Chicago, Illinois), 34-35

U
Uncle Earnie's Beer, Bait, and BBQ (Plattsmouth, Nebraska), 40-41
Uncle Willie's (Waterbury, Connecticut), 18-19
Uncle Willie's Dry Rub, 19

W
Western U.S. killer ribs, 70-89
Willow Creek Café & Saloon (Willow Creek, Montana), 72-73

Y
Yukon Ribs, Klondike's, 91

RESOURCES

In addition to *Killer Ribs*, the following books provide an excellent background and introduction to barbecue:

Peace, Love, & Barbecue: Recipes, Tall Tales, and Outright Lies from the Legends of Barbecue, by Mike Mills and Amy Mills Tunnicliffe (Rodale, 2005)

The Cook's Illustrated Guide to Grilling and Barbecue: A Practical Guide for the Outdoor Cook, by Cook's Illustrated Magazine (America's Test Kitchen, 2005)

Dinosaur Bar-B-Que: An American Roadhouse, by John Stage and Nancy Radke (Ten Speed Press, 2001)

Smokestack Lightning: Adventures in the Heart of Barbecue Country, by Lolis Eric Elie (Ten Speed Press, 2005)

ACKNOWLEDGEMENTS

Special thanks to Chris Elley, Amy Mills Tunnicliffe, Elizabeth Karmel, Adam Lang, Irene Holiastos, Nick Accardi, Kenny Callaghan, and Eric Davidson for sharing your barbecue insights and wisdom. Thanks to Andrew Davidson for sharing your office space and for your general generosity.

Thanks to Meghan Cleary and Kasey Clark of becker&mayer! for your patience and your help with photos. And of course, I am grateful to Kate Perry, my editor, for everything else.

becker&mayer! would like to thank Robb Richmond from Robb's Ribbs in Albuquerque, New Mexico, for flying up and cooking his positively delectable ribs for us.

IMAGE CREDITS

All interior photographs are courtesy of each respective restaurant, except for the following: Introduction (right to left): The Original Big Ed's BBQ, Buffalo Bob's Smokehouse, Mario Cantu for The Salt Lick, Jones Barbecue, Muddy Waters Smokehouse; page 14: Tyler Grandmaison; page 16: SBG Studio; page 30: Doug Schmidt; page 32: D.S. Heinz Art Photography; page 36: Judd Pilossof/JupiterImages; page 64: Mario Cantu; page 66: Michael Annas; page 72: Deane Mitchell; page 86: Tad Peelen; page 88: Brian Leatart/JupiterImages; page 92: Douglas Hernandez; page 102: Deborah Siu; page 104: Blade Creative Branding, Inc.

If any unintended omissions have been made, becker&mayer! would be pleased to add appropriate acknowledgements in future editions.